Contents

Chapter 1   Five Points, New York City 1

Chapter 2   'Eat 'em Up Jack' 7

Chapter 3   Children's Aid Society 13

Chapter 4   Tell Me I'm Wrong! 21

Chapter 5   The Lodging House 27

Chapter 6   Hot! 35

Chapter 7   A Welcome Place 47

Chapter 8   All Aboard! 59

Chapter 9   The Great Adventure 67

Chapter 10 Room for One More 73

Chapter 11 All Aboard! Again! 81

Chapter 12 Across Lake Erie 93

Chapter 13 Kingdom Come! 103

Chapter 14 Confession 111

Chapter 15 The Michigan Central Rail Road 119

Chapter 16 Faraway Home 129

Chapter 17 Dowagiac 139

Chapter 18 Lost! 151

Chapter 19 Poor Georgie! 163

Chapter 20 Placement 173

            Epilogue 180

i

Acknowledgements

I wish to thank the people from the Children's Aid Society, New York, New York, for sharing information concerning their organization and remaining in existence all these years for the betterment of children.

I wish to thank the members of the Orphan Train Heritage Society for all their help in my research.

I also wish to thank Doug and Tammy Bowman of St. Joseph, Michigan, for the use of their sons' names, Jack and Seth Bowman. Kristinn Blount, of Sanibel Island, Florida, for the use of her son's name (my great-nephew), Taylor Blount. Also, Jay and Annette Blount of Roanoke, Texas, for the use of their "new" daughter's name (my great-niece), Sara(h).

Most of the names of the original Orphan Train riders to Dowagiac, Michigan, have been lost to time. I used original names and scenarios when they were found and when appropriate.

A Faraway Home:
An Orphan Train Story

Janie Lynn Panagopoulos

Illustrated by
Carolyn R. Stich

EDCO Publishing, Inc.
2648 Lapeer Rd.
Auburn Hills, MI 48326
www.edcopublishing.com

First Printing 2006
Second Printing 2010

ISBN-13: 978-0-9749412-6-4

ISBN-10: 0-9749412-6-3

Library of Congress Control Number: 2005929247

Printed in the United States of America

I dedicate this book to the memory of
Charles Loring Brace and his vision for the
betterment of children.
1826-1890

Note from Author ...
Janie Lynn Panagopoulos

This book is about America and its families, generations of them who have gone without, knowing want and suffering. This book is about orphaned/homeless children who have known so much desperation and despair in their young lives that they did not know to be afraid.

This story, though fiction, is based on extensive research of the Children's Aid Society; Charles Loring Brace, its founder, and those first children who traveled from the streets of New York City to homes in the Midwest in 1854, during Charles Loring Brace's first distanced "placing-out" program.

As a mother myself, and a great supporter of education, family and home, this book was hard for me to write. I could feel for all those poor, homeless children. My teeth chattered when I read about them freezing on the streets during the cold winter months with no coats or shoes. My belly ached when I read diaries about them eating out of garbage pails and drinking hard liquor to quench their thirst; or how they were beaten, taken advantage of and physically, emotionally and sexually abused. I ached inside because I knew these tiny victims would someday grow up to be the grandparents and great-grandparents of Americans today. Our country has been built, generation after generation, on the shoulders of these hard-won victories. It is a sad story, but it also is part of our American story.

I used as much of the factual information as I was able to, being sensitive to the racial slurs and horrible, crude comments concerning children. The "common" language used on the streets in the past would be totally unacceptable for our young children today to read. The callous ways the children were used would not, today, be something that would even be legally accepted. But I did try to tell the story of these children so children today would understand the hurt and hardships of the past and appreciate what their ancestors had to go through so they can live in the manner they do today.

This isn't a pretty story. It isn't a happy story, but I was amazed how these children were able to survive with the least that life had to offer and yet continue to find happiness and companionship. The strength of these children helped me to understand why we still, today, see Americans as "survivors" of almost any hardship that is directed toward us.

"The child looks and listens, and whatsoever tone of
feeling or manner of conduct is displayed around him,
sinks into his plastic, passive soul, and becomes a mould
of his being ever ... (Children) watch us every moment,
in the family, before the hearth, and at the table; and
when we are meaning them no good or evil, when we are
conscious of exerting no influence over them, they are
drawing from us impressions and mould of habit, which,
if wrong, no patience or discipline can wholly remove;
or if right, no future exposure utterly dissipate."

-Horace Bushnell, Unconscious Influences, 1857

Children's Aid Society Circular, 1853

This society has taken its origin in the deeply settled feelings of our citizens that something must be done to meet the increasing crime and poverty among the destitute children of New York.

Its objects are to help this class by opening Sunday Meetings and Industrial Schools, and, gradually as means shall be furnished, by forming Lodging-house and Reading–rooms for children, and by employing paid agents whose sole business shall be to care for them ...

We hope, too, especially to be the means of draining the city of these children by communicating with farmers, manufacturers, or families in the country who may have need of such for employment ...

Chapter One
Five Points, New York City
Monday, September 18, 1854

"Stop! Thief! Thief!" shouted the angry voice of the Metropolitan police officer as he yanked the **billy club** from his belt. "Stop!" he demanded, raising the club high above his head and shaking it at the redheaded boy who had just escaped.

"I'll get ya, ya tough little monkey. I'll get ya and ya'll be sorry!" howled the officer as the boy pushed his way into the **gang** of street children that had begun to form.

The boy broke through the crowd and raced away down a long, narrow street of cockeyed buildings and cracked walls, leaping over heaps of **dung** and dodging **pullcarts**. Following quickly at his heels was a small, ugly dog with short, wiry legs and a spotted back. They ran side by side disappearing down a dark alley.

The officer pushed his way into the crowd of children inching the mass of bodies forward as he struggled from their clutches. They moved with him, hanging off his coat sleeves and pulling on his pant legs, slowing his pursuit of the boy, until finally he stumbled onto the **planked sidewalk.** He rammed head-on into a barrel of

1

apples and knocked it over. The deliciously red fruit tumbled from its cask like marbles pouring from a bag rolling in every direction.

Lickety-split, the gang of children broke and scattered, pushing and shoving. They grabbed at the apples, jamming them into their dirty shirts and shawls and filling their hats and pockets until they could carry no more.

"Get out of here, ya filthy thieves!" bellowed an old woman from the storefront as she swung her broom. "Of-ficer, Of-ficer! Do something! They're stealin' me apples!"

Rev. Edwin Smith watched as the **ghettoes** of New York City revealed themselves to him. It was as if he had entered into another world filled with dangerous thugs and thieves and the helplessly poor. This wasn't his world of books and education, of kindness and charity. This was a world of misery, suffering and want. The **Five Points** was the most wicked place on the most wicked streets in all of America.

Brace had sent him here to learn and understand why his plan for the homeless children of New York City was so important.

"Hey, Mister! Mister!" A small voice roused Edwin from his thoughts. "Buy a headline? Only a nickel fer the latest news. Yous look like a smart gentleman that can read ... Buy a paper fer only a nickel," said the **newsie,** who was not more than eight years old, as he smiled, gapped-toothed, and waved a paper in Edwin's face. The boy who was thin and dirty looked older than his years. His scabby hands were nearly black, stained with dirt and newspaper ink.

"Yous can read, can't ya, Mister?"

"Yes, of course I can read; however, I've already had my paper for the day. Thank you." The smile dropped

3

from the boy's face as he turned slowly away.

Taking pity on the boy, Edwin called after him. "Wait! I've changed my mind. I'll take one."

The boy turned back to Edwin and snatched the coin from his fingers while pushing a paper into his hands. "Gee, thanks, Mister!" he said with a smile.

"Do you live around here? Here in this area of Manhattan?" Surprised by the question and unsure how to answer, the little newsie paused for a moment. "I don't live nowhere, Mister," he said as he turned and ran quickly back to join his fellow newsboys, all poor and homeless, who were hoping to sell their papers so they could eat that day.

Edwin stood in the midst of the noise of carts and horses, arguing women, barking dogs, and shrieking children, thinking about how hard it must be for the children to live on the streets, alone and afraid ... "I don't live nowhere," Edwin whispered to himself. "I don't live nowhere ... "

Casting a glance across the street at a pie-sliced building that gave the Five Points its name, Edwin noticed the smudgy, redheaded boy, who had slipped from the officer's grasp just moments before, was now standing opposite of him on the corner with his pals. He munched on a stolen apple and laughed at the old woman from the store who now searched on hands and knees for any stray fruit that might have escaped the riot of children. The dirty street dog stood at his side like a snarling **sentry.**

"Buy a posy, Mister? Buy a posy?" a sweet voice asked. "I made 'em meself."

Standing before him was a barefoot girl with dirty, tangled hair who wore a patched skirt and frayed shawl. In her arms she held a broken basket filled with crumpled, pink, paper flowers.

4

"Thar just a penny, sir ... Make 'em meself. Just a penny."

"Do you go to school, child?" asked Edwin.

"Ain't no school fer me, sir. Buy a posy?"

"What about public school? You could attend there."

"No, sir. They don't want me fer me clothes are too shabby ta attend. They told me Da that."

"Do you read? Can you write your name?"

"Me Mum taught me words from the **Good Book** before she went off with the fever. Now she's gone and there's none ta teach me. Me Da can't even sign his name—but I can."

Edwin reached into his pocket, found a penny for the girl, and tossed it into her basket.

"Which flower, sir?"

"No flower. The penny is for you."

"Oh, no, sir. I can't be takin' no **charity**. Me Da wouldn't like that. Ya must take a flower or I can't take yer coin," insisted the girl as she pushed her broken basket toward him.

Surprised by her dignity, Edwin smiled, chose a crumpled paper flower, and placed it in the buttonhole of his jacket.

The girl's dark eyes lit up with pride and a smile came to her face. "It looks grand, sir."

Edwin smiled back. He would have bought all her pink paper flowers if only those pennies would have gone to buy her a hot meal or a pair of warm boots. But Brace already had warned him that these children worked for endless hours on the streets only to take money to lazy guardians who refused to work and didn't give anything, even food or a place to sleep, to the children.

And, unfortunately, this wasn't the only place. Slums spread in every direction of New York City's poor sections; **tenant buildings** were filled like honeycombs with people living **cheek-to-jowl**, waiting for the next epidemic to clean them out.

Sluggish, dirty air from coal fires, steamboats and factories gave the streets a constant haze; and the putrid stench of **slops** and overflowing **privies**, along with horse dung, roaming pigs and rotting garbage, burned at everyone's eyes and nose.

Block after block of **squalor** filled the city, and caught in the middle were the children—homeless, starving, uneducated and scared. The record, according to the chief of police, showed that over 3,000 homeless children lived alone on the streets of the Five Points.

Not ten years earlier, the Irish Potato Famine had brought nearly a million people to America. Along with the native-born children of the poor who already lived there, the **ghettoes** were overflowing. Charles Loring Brace was right; something had to be done for the children.

Chapter Two
'Eat 'em Up Jack'

A dirty hand reached out and latched onto Edwin's
sleeve, pulling him from his thoughts. "Hey, Mister.
How're ya keepin'? Buy some matches?"

"I am fine, thank you. Now, kindly remove your
hand," Edwin insisted as he looked down upon the
dirty face of the redheaded boy and his ugly dog that
now sniffed his boots. Edwin feared the boy was a
pickpocket as the Metropolitan had accused him
of being.

The boy quickly removed his hand and Edwin stamped
his foot loudly on the planked sidewalk, trying to scare
the dog away. The dog jumped but quickly came back,
snarling and showing its teeth.

"Don't mind him, Mister. He don't mean nothin',"
said the boy as he pushed the dog away. "So, hows
about buying some Lucifer sticks from me, ya know ...
some matches? Ya see, I'm a lumber merchant ...

"They call me 'Eat 'em up Jack,' cause I'm always
hungry. Why, I could butter a door 'nd eat it in one
gulp, I'm so hungry. 'nd I never likes to talk with a
hungry mouth.

"So ya gonna buy a stick of wood so I can buy a bite

of food? Five sticks fer a nickel." The boy smiled and dug deep into his tattered pants pocket, pulling out a handful of splintered wooden matches and offering them to Edwin.

"Aren't you the boy the police officer was after?"

"The purlice? Who? Me? I'm a lumber merchant, a matchseller, that's all." The boy's face was splattered with freckles and his ragged clothes fluttered in the breeze. His toes peeked from broken boots many sizes too small.

"Have you no respect for the law? For authority?" asked Edwin.

"So, Mister, ya want matches or not?"

"No. No matches for me, but I will pay for information."

"What's that? You's a Metropolitan—a purlice? Ya think I'm a **peach**? Not me. I'm honest, too. Ain't no pickpocket or liar either."

"Honest? I heard the officer call you a thief!"

"He don't know nothin'. It weren't me but another **bummer** that was pinching-a-pocket, but 'cause I was close, it was me he went after. That officer gets his coin by how many he brings in ta the station house. He doesn't care if ya did anything or not; it's just the money—that's all," said the boy as he turned and started to walk away.

"Wait, you don't understand." Edwin grabbed the boy's arm. "The information I'm looking for is only questions, questions about you and this place. I'll pay you a nickel and you can keep your matches. A lumber merchant like yourself should know a good deal when he hears one." The scraggly street dog curled back his lips, snarling at Edwin until he released the boy's arm.

"Tell your dog to stop or the deal's off!"

The boy jammed his fist of matches back into his

pocket. "I ain't no thief or liar, and it's wicked ya think so. Me Mum taught me better when she was alive. She did right by me, she did, and ya shouldn't be so wicked ta think **naught.**

"And that ain't me dog. He's like most everyone at Five Points; he belongs ta the street so I can't be tellin' him what ta do either."

Edwin listened; he could see that someplace in the boy's heart there was goodness in the midst of all this unhappiness. Even a mean dog only made friends with those who had a kind heart.

"I'm sorry. Please accept my apology. I was mistaken, that's all. It's hard to tell down here ... " Edwin stopped before he offended the boy any further and extended his hand in friendship.

"Be **gorm**, Mister, ain't never had no gentleman offered me a shake before," said the boy as he smiled and spat into his dirty fingers, rubbing the spit around to make them clean before offering his hand in return.

"I'm pleased ta make yer acquaintance, sir. I'll answer yer questions fer a nickel," said the boy as he stuck out a damp mitt to seal the deal. Startled by the boy's actions, Edwin hesitated and then took the boy's hand in his.

"Pleased to make your acquaintance, Jack. I am glad to see cleanliness is important to you. Now, son, what I want to know is do you live around here or sleep on the street? Do you go to school? Attend church? Can you read and write? Are you an orphan?"

"Gee, yer a funny one, Mister, and I ain't yer son. I gots me own Da, and he sure ain't someone like yerself. Yer a grand one ta pay me coin money to answer silly questions. Ya said ya'd pay me, but I ain't seen no coin yet." Jack tipped back onto his heels and buried his hands deep into his pockets, waiting.

9

Edwin reached into his jacket, pulled out a nickel and handed it to the boy. A great, dirty-toothed grin broke across Jack's face as he snatched up the coin, rolled it in his fingers and brought it to his lips, chomping down hard with his teeth.

"Gee, thanks, Mister. It's real," he said in appreciation. "Don't like gettin' cheated on wooden nickels, ya know."

At that instant, from behind a pullcart full of vegetables, the Metropolitan police officer, who had been after Jack before, stepped forward with his billy club in hand.

"There ya are, ya filthy little street rat!" he howled as he reached out for Jack.

"Officer, stop! There has been a mistake!" cried Edwin. "This boy didn't do anything."

The street dog, leaping to his feet, snarled and pounced on the officer's leg, bearing down hard with sharp teeth.

"Get off! Get off!" cried the officer, frantically trying to shake the dog loose. Jack, taking his chance, turned and ran as fast as he could.

Swinging his billy club at the vicious mutt, the officer missed and struck himself instead with a mighty "thud." The **cur** finally let loose and ran, chasing after Jack. The two had escaped again, this time taking Edwin's nickel and leaving his questions unanswered.

Chapter Three
Children's Aid Society
Tuesday, September 19, 1854

"There you have it. Poor children—boys, girls, orphans, half-orphans, immigrant, native born, homeless, starving, and uneducated.

"Something must be done! Those children are the future of this country!" insisted Charles Loring Brace as he sat in his office chair at the Children's Aid Society.

"Something must be done, now!" He slammed his hand down on his desk and a pile of papers fluttered into the air, like bird feathers, and floated to the floor.

"I'll get them," offered Edwin as he reached down, picking up the application forms and letters of charity.

"I'm sorry. It's just that I care for those children. They need our help! They need homes and families to love them." Brace's long, thin face was pale and beaded with sweat. He pushed back his dark hair, revealing a sharp nose and piercing eyes.

Brace, a **minister** of twenty-eight, already had traveled much of the world to learn about how other countries dealt with their homeless children. Armed with a world of knowledge, he knew there was an answer for the homeless and orphaned children of

America, too.

"So what do you think, Edwin? You're a minister. These children have need of you. Will you accompany them west?"

Edwin sat stiff in his wooden chair, thinking. Yes, he too was a minister, but this was such a great undertaking. Yet the need was there.

"It is still warm here, early autumn, but the nights are getting cooler. It has been raining and the children now are sleeping huddled together in doorways and stairwells. It is a terrible sight to see. I cannot imagine how it will be for them when winter is here. They do need to be off the streets and in decent homes."

Brace pushed back from his desk and tipped his head into his hands as he remembered the many children who had been found frozen or frostbitten on the streets the winter before.

"That was exactly why the Lodging House was started last March. To help those children by giving them a warm place to sleep and a hot meal and bath instead of letting them stand barefoot in rags in the midst of a raging winter storm. But there are thousands of these children. The Lodging Houses will not serve as the answer. We must get them permanent homes. Placing-out is the only way. Placing-out of this city and into the country with farm families is the best solution. In homes where people want them; where they can get an education and learn a **vocation.**

"The danger of ignorance is found every place that you find the poor and homeless. Do you know I spoke to nearly 500 people this week at the Five Points and could find only seven who could read or sign their own names? These people have no education, and education is the only sure means of success for their future and, at this time, they have no future."

14

"This plan of yours, Brace, is impossible. To take so many children so far in hopes of finding them homes."

"Nothing is impossible if you believe, Edwin. Now, will you help me or not? You know I would go myself if I were not needed here. All you have to do is travel with these children and keep them safely together until they arrive at their destination."

"And find them homes with strangers in a place I have never been before—with people I do not know? And why are you sending them to Michigan of all places?"

"Michigan is along the railway that leads to Chicago and the Mississippi. The railroad will help us with their transportation and fees, and there are plenty of farms and homes with good people in Michigan. If Michigan doesn't work out for placement, there always is Chicago. Edwin, the children need us ... They need you."

Edwin stared hard at Brace, thinking about the serious task that was before him. The room was silent, and the soft light from the window shown through as autumn leaves drifted aimlessly through the air to the ground below.

At that moment a heavy-fisted "bang" slammed at the office door, making both men jump.

"Are ya around in thar?" called a voice from the hall.

Startled, Brace rose from his chair and dashed to the door pulling it open just as a great brute of a man threw out his fist, nearly hitting Brace in the face. Edwin, watching, jumped to his feet in defense.

"Indeed yar here. Glad ta see it," said a tall, dirty man in a tattered shirt and pants. Unshaven and smelling with body odor, the man strutted through the door and looked around the office.

"Nearly took yar head off with that last knock, now

didn't I? Me apologizes ta ya, fine sir."

Recovering, Brace grimaced at the character. "Apology accepted. Now, how may we help you?"

Edwin stood his distance as the stink of the man's breath and body was overpowering. He wondered how Brace could stand it.

"What's that? Yar wantin' ta help me?" asked the man with his thick, Irish accent as he adjusted his suspenders. "Well, I'm glad ta hear that 'cause it is yar help I am in need of." The man scratched himself and turned, looking suspiciously out into the hallway behind him.

"Boy! Get in here!" he bellowed.

Brace turned to Edwin and shrugged his shoulders not knowing what to expect. A small, low voice from outside in the hall responded. "No, Da, please!"

"Ya heard me!" thundered the man. "Now don't get saucy with me and get through this door!" The dirty, slouched-shoulder, unwashed man turned into the hall, pulling the door closed behind him. Outside, a clamor of commotion was heard. Brace yanked the door open just in time to see the man grabbing hold of a boy who tried to make his escape down the staircase.

"Here now, stop manhandling that child. We will have none of that here, sir!" insisted Brace.

"Get in here now!" roared the man as he pulled the boy through the doorway and into the office.

"Here! Take him!" he said pushing the child across the room into Edwin's arms.

Shocked, Edwin stared down at the boy and recognized him as the redheaded lumber merchant, Jack, from the streets the day before.

"Is this your son, sir?" demanded Brace.

"The lad's mine, he is. But I can't keep him no more. The cough took his Mum last spring, and I can't keep him no more. I can't. I heard ya take children in. Take care of 'em, feed and clothe 'em? Well, I can't do none of that; can't even do it for meself. "I ain't got no job, no money, no food. I thought maybe I'd go west and try me hand panning fer gold in California or workin' the rails."

"Take me with ya, Da!" begged Jack as he moved away from Edwin, his eyes red, swollen, and blind with tears.

"Quiet! Now don't make it harder on the both of us. I've made up me mind."

"Da?" pleaded the boy. "Please ..."

"Well, will ya take him or not? Ya know what I mean—take care of him, get 'im an education, find 'im a decent place ta live. Away from the streets and all the trouble he gets 'imself inta. I never got meself an education, never got meself nothing but trouble. I want more fer the lad. His Mum would have wanted that, too."

Edwin reached out and touched Jack's arm. The boy shuddered and pulled away, snot dripping from his nose onto the floor.

"We will take him, sir," interrupted Edwin. "We will take him."

"Then he's yars! 'nd don't let me hear ya've been mistreatin' the lad or there'll be a price ta pay, ya hear? Now, show me where ta sign."

Edwin placed his arms around Jack's shoulders and helped the sobbing boy to a chair. Jack's body was full of anger and defiance. His lips quivered with hurt, and tears flowed in muddy streaks down his dirty face.

Brace closed the office door quietly and shuffled through the scattered papers on his desk until he found the form that was needed. He placed it before the man with a pen and inkpot.

17

"You should read this before you sign."

"I told ya. I can't read or write. Just show me where ta make me mark. I trust ya."

"Please, Da. Let me go west with ya. We could find a pile of gold, just the two of us. Ya'd need me fer that ta count all the millions we'd be pilin' up."

"Hush now!" snapped the man as he scratched an inky X on the form, turning the responsibility of his son over to the Children's Aid Society.

"That be all?"

"Yes, sir. That's all. You know, unless your son is adopted or placed-out, you can come see him. Anytime you want, we will take you to him," informed Brace.

"Perhaps. We'll see how it goes." The man turned to his son and grabbed hold of his chin in his rough hand, pulling the boy's face upward.

"Ya behave yarself, ya hear? I'm doing this fer yar own good. Ya don't want ta be turning out as worthless 'nd ignorant as yar old man now, do ya? Make something of yarself. When ya get to be a great man, I'll come look ya up!"

Tears again streaked down the boy's dirty face as he watched his father leave the office. The stomping of his heavy boots echoed on the stair steps and finally faded away with the slam of the outside door.

The room was silent now except for the boy's sniffles. Brace reached into his pocket and pulled out a handkerchief, offering it to him. Jack sat there silent and motionless and slowly lifted his eyes to look clearly at the two of them. Pushing the handkerchief aside, he rubbed his bloodshot eyes with dirty hands and wiped his nose on his shirtsleeve.

Soon, his eyes grew wide as he recognized Edwin. Filled with rage, he jumped up, knocking over the chair and pushing the men aside, as he scrambled for an escape.

Brace grabbed the door and held it shut while Edwin grabbed Jack who fought and struggled, swinging his legs and fists.

"Let me go! Let me go! Murderers! Murderers! I'll have the Metropolitans after ya if ya don't let me go!"

Edwin held tight as Jack kicked and fought until he exhausted himself in anger and collapsed onto the floor in tears of frustration.

Charles Loring Brace and Edwin Smith stood silently over the boy, watching—waiting. Edwin cleared his throat and blew his nose, hurting for the boy but knowing that Jack's father had done the right thing for him. Something that wasn't easy.

Patting Edwin on the back, feeling his compassion, Brace knew this was the right man to take the orphans west.

Chapter Four
Tell Me I'm Wrong!

"Are you hungry?" Edwin asked, stooping down trying to make friends and soothe the boy's broken heart. "Would you like something to eat?"

Jack looked up in anger and snapped, "Ya know I'm hungry. I'm always hungry. I told ya that yesterday; Ya know me names 'Eat 'em up Jack'."

"Yesterday, I thought ya were the purlice, but now I know yar worse. Ya came lookin' fer me yesterday, didn't ya? But I was too slick fer ya. Now tell me I'm wrong."

"You're wrong, Jack," said Edwin.

"You know this boy?"

"Ya, he knows me. Yar gonna send me ta Blackwell's Island, the prison, aren't ya? Tell me I'm wrong."

"You're wrong, Jack," insisted Edwin.

"You know this boy?" asked Brace again as he walked to his desk, pulled open a drawer, and found an apple which he offered to the boy.

Jack snatched the apple from Brace's hand and threw it hard against the wall, smashing it into pieces in his rage. The sticky mess oozed down the wall.

"Just tell me again I'm wrong. I dare ya!"

21

"Well, I see you don't like apples," commented Brace, shocked by the boy's actions.

"Oh, he likes apples well enough. Don't you, Jack?" Edwin interrupted. "Why, I watched you eat a stolen one just yesterday down at the Five Points."

"So is this what ya do when ya get a nickel pinched and an apple stolen?" Jack wiped a stream of snot from his nose onto his hand.

Edwin winced and pulled the handkerchief from his pocket and dropped it into the boy's lap. Balling it up, Jack threw it back. "I don't want nothin' from ya."

"So you two met at the Five Points?"

"Yes, that's where we met."

"What an incredible coincidence."

Edwin raised his eyebrows and took in a deep breath. "Yes, I agree."

"This is Jack or 'Eat 'em up Jack,' as he prefers to be called. Jack, this is Mr. Charles Loring Brace. He is head of the Children's Aid Society." Not wanting to acknowledge the introduction, Jack cast his eyes to the floor.

"So what shall we do with him? We have no housing for him here."

"No, no, of course not. We will take him to the Lodging House. Mr. Tracy and his assistants will get him cleaned up and get the lice and the fleas off his body before the evening meal.

"A hot evening meal, Jack. Did you hear that? A good, hot, evening meal with three slices of bread if you like and a double serving of stew if you please," said Brace as he stooped to the boy, trying to make him understand that they only wanted to help.

"You will even get a hot bath. When was the last time you had a hot bath, Jack? Can you remember?"

Jack looked up blankly and stared at Brace's sharp

features. "I ain't never had a hot bath before, not that I can remember. At least, not a full dippin'."

"Well, you'll have a hot bath tonight," added Edwin. "There will be other children there, too, just like you."

"What ya mean like me?" Jack glared at Edwin still not trusting him yet.

"Children who are homeless. Children who want and need better lives. Children who are getting an education and earning their own keep. You will make lots of friends there," said Brace.

"I don't need no more friends. I got plenty of friends and only one Da, but now he's gone. Gone for good no doubt. He never was around when I needed him, and now he's sold me out.

" 'Sides, I don't have money ta pay fer anything fancy like what yer talkin' about. I can't pay nothing. Except ..." The boy rose to his knees and, reaching into his pants pocket, pulled out a fistful of matches and Edwin's nickel.

"Not to worry. You don't need to pay anything for your keep. Not until you're trained and working or perhaps even placed-out."

"Now wait, Brace. This young man is a lumber merchant; you can see his matches. He knows the worth of money.

"Didn't you tell me the other children pay six cents a night for a hot bath and a bed and another four cents for a hot meal? That is ten cents a night for room and board. Am I correct?"

"Yes, but this is different. I don't see ... "

"Well, since this young man has a nickel, I think we should let him start now helping to pay his way," insisted Edwin as he plucked his coin out of the boy's dirty hand and gave it to Brace for safekeeping.

"Well, I suppose every nickel Mr. Tracy receives is

23

helpful if that is alright with you, Jack?"

Jack slowly nodded his head in agreement. He pulled himself to his feet and dusted off his trousers, running his fingers through his snarled red hair. "I might as well go with ya; ain't got no better offers, 'nd me Da don't care no more.

"Ya say they're gonna get rid of me lice and fleas? They eat at me something awful, ya know."

"Yes, Mr. Tracy will want to make sure that you aren't carrying any personal vermin. No lice, fleas or bed bugs are welcome at Mr. Tracy's Lodging House. It is a clean house that he and his wife keep."

"Well, I suppose it'll be alright ta stay thar. That is, in case me Da changes his mind and comes lookin' fer me so he'll know where ta find me. He's gonna make a fortune in the gold fields out west, ya know. Ya heard him say that, didn't ya?"

Slowly, the three of them made their way down to the street into the whitewashed world of prosperous New York City. It wasn't anything like the streets Jack was used to which were full of broken houses and broken people.

Chapter Five
The Lodging House

As the three of them walked, they passed by **buggies** filled with fancy ladies dressed in frilly dresses and men in top hats and suits. There was no garbage to walk around or threatening jeers of street thugs to listen to. To Jack, it was as if he had stepped into another world.

The eyes of the row houses were clean and shiny, and lace curtains hung neatly in each one. Jack didn't even see a window that was broken or cracked. There were window boxes filled with golden autumn flowers and smiles on the faces of all that he passed. It was a beautiful sight to see.

"You will like Mr. Tracy and the Lodging House. Mr. Tracy is a fine man," said Brace sincerely.

"This Tracy sounds like he has a nice place, but he's not runnin' a thieves' lodge is he? I've been thar before with me Da. Thar mean and wicked places like the one on Rotten Row. I learned more about putting me hand in someone's pocket or purse than I ever learned on the streets.

"But I always remembered what me poor old Mum said. She is gone now, ya know. She got herself sick. They buried her in Potter's Field, 'cause we were too

27

poor ta have a place fer her." Jack paused as he could feel the tears again starting to burn in his eyes. "It's a shame, not ta have a place fer yar Mum, not even a stone ta visit.

"Me Mum ..." Jack swallowed hard, "she said thieving is no way ta make a livin'.

"Me Mum was good ta me, ya know, 'nd I don't ever want ta make her ashamed of me, even though she's in her grave now." Tears started to tumble down Jack's dirty, freckled cheeks as he quickly wiped them away on his sleeve and continued to walk.

Brace looked at the boy feeling his hurt and thinking of his own mother. Reaching out, he grabbed Jack by the shoulder bringing the boy to a halt. "Jack," he said stooping down and looking seriously into his eyes, "you are a good boy with a good heart and I know your mother could never be ashamed of you. I am sure you will grow up to be a very fine young man. All you need is some help."

Surprised by Brace's kind words, Jack was silent and swallowed hard. Edwin patted Jack on the shoulder and nodded his head yes in agreement.

"Did ya hear what he said ta me? Did ya hear it? A grand man like this said those kind words about me? Ain't no one said nothin' like that before."

"It's true, Jack," added Edwin. "You are a right thinker. You will make something of yourself if you keep doing the right things and making the right choices."

Brace smiled at Jack, and Edwin was pleased, too, knowing that he had recognized the decency in the child the day before when they had first met.

"Can we get movin' now? I want ta feel meself in a dish of hot water, plunged in up ta me neck, drownin' all those nasty vermin that chews on me hide. None of the boys would ever believe ya could have a hot bath and a hot meal, both on the same day."

Brace smiled at Edwin as the three walked in the cool autumn air, crunching fallen leaves in their path until the Lodging House came into view. It was a big, brick building with four floors and many windows.

Jack, uncertain about what adventure was about to follow, stayed close to Edwin and Brace as they unlatched the black, iron gate. It creaked open, showing the walkway and the double-entry doors of the Lodging House.

Jack wondered if he should make a final attempt to escape. After all, he had heard stories from the streets of torture and pirates in these types of places, but he had paid a nickel for the night and the idea of a hot meal, a clean bed and stewing in a bath of hot water was too much of a temptation. It would all be worth it even if he did get **shanghaied** by pirates and taken to the South Seas.

"Are you coming in?" asked Edwin.

Slowly, Jack entered through the heavy doors. The long, wide hallway was filled with a warm glow of light that came from the large windows at the end of the hall. The light reflected from the polished wooden floor, casting shadows behind Brace as he walked swiftly ahead and disappeared through a doorway.

Jack stopped and stared at the beauty of the place.

"What's wrong?"

"The floor ... It looks like water it's so shiny. I ain't never seen nothin' like it before. It looks just like the shimmerin' on the ocean down by the docks."

"Yes, Mr. Tracy and his wife keep a very clean place here. You're right. It does look like water, but you won't fall in. It's fine to walk on ... just follow me."

"'Tis a thing of beauty."

Edwin smiled and led the way. Brace poked his head

29

out from the doorway where he had entered, motioning for them to hurry along.

The room where Brace stood was an office filled with shelves of books and a small desk. Sitting behind the desk was a short, round man with a kind face and a large smile.

"Glad you will be staying with us here for a while," said the man when Jack entered. "I understand you might be a candidate for our train west that will be leaving soon."

"Train west? Me Da's gone west. Ya mean I'll be jonin' me Da in the gold fields?"

"Jack," interrupted Brace. "This is Mr. Tracy."

Tracy, not knowing what Jack meant, was surprised by the boy's comments.

"No, Jack, son ..." said Brace ... "Mr. Tracy doesn't mean west to the gold fields; he means west to Michigan."

"I ain't yar son. I got me a Da, ya met 'im. He just can't take care of me anymore, that's all. I am only a half-orphan. 'nd this Mich-i-gan, what's that?"

"I only meant to tell you that Mr. Smith is helping Mr. Brace organize an expedition—an adventure west—to find good homes for all you fine children. You and some of the others will be on that trip and it is heading westward."

"I ain't here fer no trip. Just a hot bath 'nd ta get me lice picked and fleas drowned. If I go west, it'll be ta find me Da."

"Jack, your father wanted us to find you a good home; you heard him say that. A home where you can live with a good family, get an education and be cared for."

"I knew ya'd shanghai me." Jack's emotions were all stirred up again.

"Ya got me here with the promise of a warm bath and a hot meal and now I'm shanghaied. 'Tis the end of me. I knew it. Ya can't trust none of ya fancy men." Jack turned suddenly and started for the door. "I've changed me mind! I don't want ta stay," he demanded, his voice filled with mistrust and anger.

"Jack, you will get your hot meal and a bath and a warm, dry bed. You will get all those things just as we promised," insisted Brace as he stood before the door, blocking Jack's way.

"But we want to make sure," added Edwin, "that you have those things every day for the rest of your life. In a place you can call home."

"Home. I don't even know what the word means. It don't mean nothin' ta me. I ain't had a home since me Mum's been gone." Tears flowed down Jack's cheeks as the fear crept back into him like icy fingers.

"Home is a good thing, Jack," said Edwin as he reached out to the boy.

"Just give it a try. If it doesn't work, you can come back here to New York City and the Lodging House. You don't need to be afraid. I will go with you, traveling all the way to Michigan to help you and all the other children find homes of your own. We will travel on the train. It will be a great adventure, Jack." Brace looked at Edwin, catching his eye, and smiled. The boy had won him over, and Edwin now was committed to take the orphans west.

Mr. Tracy reached out, putting his arm around Jack's shoulder. "We want to help you. Please let us try."

Tears ran down Jack's face. He had been tired, hungry and dirty for such a long time, and the idea of having a safe place off the streets and perhaps even a home was hard for him to accept or even understand.

"Now, say good-bye to Rev. Brace and Rev. Smith. You

will be seeing them in just a few days' time when you start on your adventure with the other children."

Charles Loring Brace extended his hand. "You take care of yourself, Jack, and do exactly as Mr. Tracy tells you. You will do just fine. I believe in you."

Jack looked into Brace's eyes, knowing he had never met such a kind man as this before. Jack took his hand and squeezed it tight, wishing it wasn't good-bye.

"Jack …," interrupted Edwin. "I am so very glad I will have you aboard for our great adventure. I will be counting on you to help with the other children. Will that be fine with you?"

A small smile came to Jack's dirty, tear-streaked face. He had never been needed before. "Ya, I suppose ya can count on me, Mister," he said as they shook hands.

"Alright then, Jack, let us go upstairs and get you bathed, dressed and ready for a hot meal and bed."

"That sounds grand ta me." Jack looked over his shoulder to Brace and Edwin, wiped his nose on his shirtsleeve, and then smiled a good-bye.

Mr. Tracy led Jack down the hall, past the dining room, and up the stairs to his new life.

Chapter Six
Hot!

Following Mr. Tracy upstairs, Jack was amazed by how clean and shiny everything was. There were no rags or piles of trash, no slop jars filled to the rim, nor anyone sleeping crumpled in the corner on the floor. He had never seen anything like it. Shivers ran up his arms.

On the second-floor landing, a pretty woman dressed in a green flowered dress and white apron passed by them and smiled.

"Oh, my dear, I would like you to meet our new guest ... This is Jack. Jack, this is my wife, Mrs. Tracy."

Jack smiled at the pretty woman, admiring her. She, too, was clean. Her hair was neatly gathered in braids around her head. She even had all her front teeth, which were white and even, a sight rarely seen at the Five Points.

"Oh, my; it looks as if you will be needing some hot water and new clothes and boots," she said as she sized up Jack.

"That was just what I was thinking. Could you please see to it?"

"I would be happy to, and welcome, Jack." Jack smiled back at Mrs. Tracy and stared at her as she went down the staircase.

"Come along, Jack," Mr. Tracy said, "There are plenty of other things to look at here in the Lodging House."

Soon, shouting and yelling voices echoed down the long, wide hall. It was as if a hundred screaming cats were trying to escape a pack of wild dogs. Jack stopped and wondered what horrible thing was happening to make such a noise. "What's that?"

"What's what? You mean the boys?" asked Mr. Tracy as he walked to two tall, wooden doors and swung them open. It was a great room filled with boys who were laughing, playing, throwing balls and chasing one another. The room echoed with laughter and happiness. Jack had never heard or seen anything like that.

"Mr. Tracy, how's ya doin?" called a voice.

"Mr. Tracy! Who's the new boy?" called another.

"Hey, Mr. Tracy, come play ball."

In the sea of faces, Jack thought he recognized boys he once knew from the streets who were thought to have been shanghaied by pirates or to have met a fate even worse than that. But here they were—alive, well and happy.

"It is exercise, Jack. This is a gymnasium," Mr. Tracy said as he closed the doors to help keep the sounds of delight within. "Here we have exercise for the mind, body and spirit; they all are important."

Jack had never heard the word "exercise" before, but he knew it was something he was going to like.

Around the corner, they entered a large room with tiled walls and many large tin tubs surrounded by screens. Along the wall were washing bowls and empty pitchers waiting for water.

"This is our washroom where you will have your bath." I want you to remove all your clothes behind the screen and leave them on the floor. I will dispose

36

of them for you. We don't want to be spreading your personal vermin to any of the other boys, now do we? Make sure you have all your personal items out of the pockets because you will not be seeing these things again, and we will be giving you different clothes after your bath." Mr. Tracy pulled the screen around Jack to give him his privacy while he undressed. It had been early summer since Jack had had his clothes off. He had followed a gang of street pals down to the docks and taken a dip in the cold, salty ocean. That was the only kind of bath Jack had known.

"I think these will fit him fine. What do you think, dear?" asked Mrs. Tracy as she entered the room. Jack, who was skinned down to his dirty, holey long johns, stood half naked, frozen to the spot.

"Yes, those will do just fine. They look like they will fit a twelve-year-old boy. Thank you."

Jack pulled his tattered pants out of the dirty, crumpled pile on the floor and yanked them on for fear Mrs. Tracy might see him. Reaching into his pocket, he nervously ran his fingers through his splintered matches, pulling them out. As he stared down at the matches, he wondered if he should keep them.

Removing five matches, just enough to buy a nickel meal, Jack put them on the window sill, setting them aside for the future, just in case. The rest he let fall from his fingers like washing away the dirt of the street. Getting new clothes, he now hoped for a new and better life.

"Once you are undressed, Jack," called Mrs. Tracy, "please get into the empty tub. Hurry along. We are waiting."

Jack stood for a moment and looked around. Behind him sat a large, empty, tin tub. Big enough for Jack to stretch out in and have a real soak, but ...

"Ma'me, will it be you that gives me a scrubbin'?"

"Oh, Jack, don't be silly. Of course not. I just brought you your clothes. Now hurry along. Get undressed and into the tub."

Jack sighed with relief, dropped his pants, and removed his dirty long johns. Carefully, he lowered himself, naked, into the cold, tin tub.

"Here we go, Jack," said Mr. Tracy. "I can hear Mary coming down the hall with the cart of hot water. Mary will help you scrub out the lice and drown those nasty fleas." The squeaky wheels of a cart could now plainly be heard coming down the hall, closer and closer.

Shocked, Jack didn't know what to do. He had no plans for any person with a woman's name to be seeing him naked. Struggling out of the tub, he reached for his pile of clothes just as Mr. Tracy's hand slipped under the screen to pull them away. Jack grabbed and tugged for his holey long johns, freeing them and, quick-as-a-wink, pulled them on. He jumped back into the empty tub and scrunched up in the bottom of the tank. He waited.

The squeaky wheels of the cart entered the vacant, tiled room and sang their own tune across the floor. Jack listened as the sweet sound of an Irish woman's voice was heard.

"Oh, look, it is both the Mister and the Misses. Now ain't that a pretty picture? I have plenty of hot water fer our new lodger. Is he ready for his scrubbin'?"

"Yes, Mary. Here are his soap, scrub brush, towel, clothes and boots. Now, he will need to be scrubbed top to bottom and the lice combed from his hair and no fleas left hopping ... And, Mary, please, make sure you don't scrub too hard. Remember what happened last time."

Last time? What did that mean? Jack drew his legs

close to his chest and wrapped his arms tightly around them.

"Oh, Mrs. Tracy, ya know me hands don't scrub like they used ta. I'm very gentle. Ya know that, Misses."

"Yes, I know, but no more boys coming out looking like red lobsters. Do you understand, Mary?"

"Yes, Misses, I do."

"Fine then. The boy is waiting for you. We will be down the hall if you need us."

Jack sat with his face buried in his knees as he listened to the quick footsteps belonging to Mr. and Mrs. Tracy fade away down the hall. Mary's cart squeaked again as she pulled back the screen and guided it next to the washtub. Jack wondered if all this really was worth a full dippin' in hot water.

Slowly he raised his head and stared head-on at one of the largest women he had ever seen. She must have been rich, as Jack had never seen such a well-fed woman in all his days at the Five Points. She was tall as well as wide and wore a great, gray dress with a white cap on her head that made her look like the paintings of mountains he had seen hanging in the storefronts. Her hair was wiry and gray, and she had three chins that wobbled with each step she took.

"So, what do we have here?" she said, as she glanced down at Jack and realized he was still in his long johns.

Jack tightened his face and stared up from the bottom of the tub, daring her to say anything against him.

"What's yar name, boy?" she demanded in a threatening tone, her hands on her massive hips. She was worse than a pirate, thought Jack.

"I said, what's yar name, boy? I'm Mary and I'll be helpin' ya with yar tub."

"Jack ... Jack ... me name is Jack."

39

"Oh, I hear a bit of Irish on yar tongue. Thar's lots of us here. Now, Jack, ya mind tellin' me how it is I'm suppose ta scrub ya top ta bottom wearing long johns so dirty and holey a rag picker wouldn't want them? Jump out of that tub and strip ta yar skin, so I can get ya clean."

"No, Ma'me."

"What's that ya'd be sayin'? Did I hear ya tell me no?"

Jack swallowed hard, "It's just ... just ... "

"Oh, it's just I'm a woman and ya don't want me ta be seeing ya naked as a jaybird. Is that it?"

Jack nodded his head yes and buried his face in his knees in embarrassment.

"Well, I see. I guess we can work around that. I wasn't wantin' ta get down on me hands and knees fer ya anyways. So, I suppose ya will have ta scrub yarself. But if ya don't get it right, I'll have ta do it for ya. The Tracys are particular people. They don't like no dirty children in thar lodgin' house.

"Ya hear me?"

Jack glanced up at Mary. "I hear ya."

"Now, don't make me get down on me hands as I already have had a long day, and I'm not up to no nonsense from ya. So do it right the first time."

"I promise."

"All right. Then let's get at it. I still have ta fill the tub."

Mary reached for her cart filled with large pitchers of water—some steaming, some not. "Ya ready?"

Sitting up straight and stretching out his legs in front of him, Jack nodded his head yes and waited for the nice streams of warm water from the pitchers to cover over his body.

Mary lifted one of the steaming jugs and, standing

over Jack, she quickly poured the water over his head and body.

Jack stiffened and arched forward. Letting out a howl, he jumped from the tub carrying half the water with him out onto the floor.

"What ya tryin' ta do ta me? Boil me like a **pratty** in a cooker?"

"Don't be sassin' me none, boy. Now look what ya've done, ya rotten scoundrel, pullin' all that water from the tub. You'll be cleanin' that mess up when yar done. Now get back in the tub."

"Not in boilin' water I'm not ... Do I look like tea?"

"Well, as brown as this water is already with just a little dunkin', yar could be mistaken fer tea. Now get back in the tub."

"Put the water in and let it cool," demanded Jack.

"Oh, ya sound like the Prince of England. Get in the tub!"

"What is going on in here, Mary? I could hear the two of you all the way down the hall." It was Mr. Tracy. He stared at Mary who was still holding a steaming pitcher in her hand and at Jack, who stood silently, dripping, soaked clear to the skin in his holey long johns.

"You two certainly are a sight. Mary, how many times have we told you that you can't be scalding the boys?"

"She said she thought she was makin' tea of me. I think she was tryin' ta boil me like a pratty."

"Wouldn't be no tea ya'd be wantin' ta drink, sir."

"Well, I am sure of that. Now, Mary, fill the tub with both the hot and cold water before the boy gets in.

"And, Jack, I want you to get out of those filthy long johns. Do you understand, young man?"

"Yes, sir."

"Mary?"

"Yes, sir. It's just this boy has made such an awful mess now and ..."

"Mary, fill the tub."

"Yes, sir."

Jack and Mr. Tracy watched as the tub was mixed with both the hot and cold water and the steam curled into the air, making an inviting stew pot for a soak.

"That should be fine for the boy, sir. He said he wanted ta scrub on his own. Tell the boy ta scrub good or I'll have ta come back ta help him."

"Yes, Mary, thank you. You may leave now."

The squeaky wheels of the cart sang a different tune now that it was empty of its steaming load. The empty water pitchers rattled, one against the other, in accompaniment.

"Well, Jack. Our Mary is quite something, isn't she? But you did hear what she said about scrubbing up properly? Or she'll be back and she will nearly scrub the hide off you, until you look as shiny as the day you were born. Understand?"

Jack stood wide-eyed and wet. This must have been what they meant on the streets when the boys talked about the tortures that took place in the Lodging House.

"I understand."

After Mr. Tracy left, Jack peeled out of his holey long johns and eased himself into the tub. The water rose nearly to his chest as he sat back. He never had felt anything like this before. It was like lying in a cloud on a warm, sunny day. Like floatin' in the ocean down by the docks, only the water wasn't salty or cold and there weren't any nasty, dead things floating around him. He closed his eyes, enjoying the moment.

In the distance he heard heavy footsteps approaching. Then a cool rush of air filled the room and, "whap," just from behind the screen Mary appeared with a great mop.

"Hey, what ya doin'? Sit up and get scrubbed!"

Jack sat up quickly and hid himself as Mary sloshed the mop over the floor, picking up the splashed water and wringing it into a bucket.

"Here's yar soap and brush. Get scrubbin'."

She tossed a hard square of yellowish soap into the tub followed by a long-handled brush. They both splashed more water out onto the floor.

"Scrub!"

Jack fished around to find the soap and brush and rubbed them together, making a pile of soap bubbles that covered the clear water.

"Wash every bit of ya including yar back, neck and ears." Mary wrung out the mop and danced it across the floor again to pick up the last splashes.

"What are these? These yars?"

Jack turned; Mary was holding his five matches. "Are these yars, I asked?"

"Yes, Ma'me."

"For yar future? Just in case?"

Jack nodded.

"Well, ya must be smarter than ya look. Ya can never be too certain about yar future, and it's always best ta put somethin' aside, just in case. I'll put 'em back on the sill. Don't be forgettin' them. Ya hear?"

"Yes, Ma'me."

Jack watched as Mary waddled out with her mop and bucket. She was like so many other women from the city—no nonsense and as tough as nails, but underneath she knew how hard life really was and was on his side.

Jack dunked his head and scrubbed his body over and over with the brush. He scrubbed his ears and neck, even his back where no one but Mary would ever see or look. After that, he scrubbed his feet and legs until

44

every inch of him was cleaner than it ever had been before.

Rising quickly from the tub, he dried off and dressed, slipping his matches into his pocket.

Chapter Seven
A Welcome Place

When Mary returned, she combed his hair with a
tiny comb in search of lice and inspected his neck and
ears. Pleased with his scrubbing, she buttoned the top
button on his shirt with her big, sausage fingers and
straightened his suspenders. His clothes, though not
new, smelled of soap and starch and had no holes.
The soles of his lace-up boots held his feet snug and
tight against leather, and nothing flapped loose when
he walked.

Jack felt new all over. It was an odd feeling for
someone who never had anything in his life.

Mr. Tracy soon returned and led Jack to the dining
hall on the first floor where row after row of long tables
were filled with hungry, noisy boys who eagerly were
waiting for their meal.

The wonderful smells reminded Jack of the eatery
places where he had begged outside for pennies from
rich **patrons** and where he would wait in the alleyways
near the eatery's back door for discarded food scraps
to eat.

On the tables were plates of thick-sliced bread, dishes
of butter, and bowls of steaming stew piled high with
potatoes, carrots, onions and chunks of meat.

47

Mr. Tracy found a place for Jack at the end of a table and then proceeded up the aisle to a head table where he stood silently in front of the boys while waiting with his wife for the clamor of voices to quiet.

Soon the room grew silent, and a hundred chairs scratched and were pushed back from the tables as the boys stood. A hand quickly reached out and yanked Jack by his shirt collar to his feet. It was Mary. She squinted a glance at him, folded her hands and bowed her head. Jack looked around to see the boys doing the same.

Mr. Tracy cleared his throat and in a very loud voice delivered a blessing on the boys and thanks for the food. His voice was clear and strong, and it echoed through the hall. A chill ran up Jack's spine. He didn't know what it all meant, but the words were beautiful and made him feel grateful for being here. The instant Mr. Tracy finished, the room exploded in sound with chairs being pulled in, dishes passed, stew slurped and spoons clanking on teeth.

"Hey, bummer! Pass the budder," demanded a voice.

"Hey, yous, pass the budder! What's da matter? Ya ain't never seen budder?" Jack, so caught up in the wonderful flavor of the stew and filling his belly, didn't realize anyone was speaking to him. A sharp elbow next to him jabbed Jack in the side.

"Hey, watch it."

"Pass the butter down," whispered the small boy beside him.

Just then a large hand slammed down on the table beside Jack. "Don't ya know thars ta be no talkin', slurpin' or belchin' at the table unless ya want somthin' passed?" demanded Mary. "Don't be makin' trouble in the dinin' hall or ya will go ta bed hungry. Do ya understand?"

Jack nodded his head yes and slowly reached for the

butter dish, passing it down the row.

"I didn't know he was talkin' ta me," whispered Jack to the boy beside him.

The boy looked up from his food and smiled. He was small and young, maybe only six or seven. His feet didn't even touch the floor when he sat, and they swang continuously while he ate.

"Shhh ... " whispered the boy. "Don't let Mary catch ya talking. She will be after us all. I'm George."

Jack smiled, "Thanks. Yar a pal."

The small boy grinned silently.

Jack ate until he thought his belly would burst. He never had eaten so much food in all of his life; and it was good food, filling food, food that would stick to his ribs. He washed it all down with buttermilk, which was

a rare treat.

Soon Mr. Tracy rose. The boys pushed their bowls back and put their spoons down. Everyone stood at Mr. Tracy's signal and filed into rows in the aisle. Everything was done with silent precision and Jack, being at the head of his row, was pushed along by George to follow after the boys ahead of him.

"Where we going?"

"To the auditorium for the evening program." Silently and obediently, boy after boy moved along in line with their bellies full and stew stains on their shirts and buttermilk mustaches on their faces.

"Come on! Get a move on," insisted George, pushing Jack forward into the boys. "Just follow everyone else. We want to sit in the front if ya want ta hear anything." Jack moved forward and followed into a large room filled with benches. Once inside, the rows of boys broke order and everyone scrambled for familiar seats next to chums, jumping over benches and pushing each other aside.

George yanked Jack by the arm onto a bench close to the front of the room.

Mr. Tracy entered and stood waiting for the boys to find their places and for the room to become quiet. Mary stood with her great arms crossed over her chest and shot nasty glances across the room to anyone who looked as if they wanted to have too much fun.

Jack looked around and watched the boys, some poking and pinching and others giving the elbow to their seat partners. Here and there the sound of a belch or the breaking of wind could be heard, and then a wave of laughter and joking remarks filled the air.

Mr. Tracy stood silently and waited until all was calm and under control. He looked to the back of the room toward Mary and nodded, and with that signal she exited and closed the big wooden doors behind her.

"Good evening, boys, and welcome to those of you who are new. As most of you know, after each evening at the Newsboys Lodging House, we have a time of sharing. I know not all of you are newsboys. Some are boot blacks and errand runners; some hold horses, sell matches and have various jobs on the streets. But all of you, at one time or another, probably have slept in a barrel, in a doorway or under a stairway in dirty clothes and with empty bellies. But there is none of that here tonight, is there? Are all your bellies full?"

The boys responded with wild applause and whistles.

"I know there are some of you here tonight who know more at the age of twelve than the children of ordinary men would have learned at twenty. You are very special young men with many things to offer the world. Isn't that true?"

The room again filled with applause and then quieted. Jack looked around and noticed that some of the boys continued to nod their heads in agreement, eager to hear Mr. Tracy's words. Some had their hands in their pockets and legs stretched out relaxed while others scooted back on their bench with their arms crossed, a hard look on their faces. But everyone had his head up and eyes fully on Mr. Tracy and, without an exception, their mouths closed tightly.

"I want you to know this is a welcoming place. A place of goodwill. A place where you can learn a trade, receive an education and start your lives over. That is why we take turns sharing our stories and our tales, and I was wondering whom you choose tonight to deliver your **oratory?**"

Jack looked around and George nudged him with his elbow and whispered. "Paddy is a good one ta tell a story. Call for Paddy."

"Hows about Paddy?" came a loud voice from the back of the room.

"Ya, Paddy, tell us a story," cried another.

"Paddy, Paddy, Paddy," the voices chanted around the room, and George and Jack joined in.

"Paddy," called Mr. Tracy. "Why don't you show yourself. Your friends are calling for you."

From the back of the room, a short, freckled-faced boy made his way to the front of the room climbing over legs and receiving pats on the back from his pals. He was no older than Jack, with dark, round eyes and a short, snubbed nosed. When he reached the front of the room, Mr. Tracy offered him a chair, and Paddy positioned it just right before he hopped up upon the seat for all to see.

"Bummers, snoozers, wildcats, and citizens of all sorts," he said in a loud, commanding voice. "You all have asked me ta speak ta ya a little this evening 'bout the way things are. To encourage ya ta be better. I know there are some of ya who stand at the pie shops with yar nose ta the window, smellin' all the good things that are there ta offer—all ya fellers who's got no homes, no food, no money."

Snickers and laughter filled the room. "Oh, Paddy, yar full of gas!" called a boy, laughing at his pal.

George looked up and grinned at Jack. "He's funny, this one. He's real funny."

"I call ya bummers, cause yar all bummers. I once was a bummer until these kind people, the Tracys, took me in. They gave me an education and taught me a better way ta do life.

"I have hopes for ya all like I gots hopes for me. I want ya ta grow up to be rich men, prosperous men, men with food on yar table and a roof over yar heads. Just like I will be. If I can do it, I know we all can do it. Are ya with me on that?"

Here and there the boys clapped in support.

"Oh, dry up, Paddy. Yar still a bummer in a Lodgin' House."

"Put a bag over yar head, Paddy."

"Well, boys, let me tell ya me story. One beautiful day I slipped away from me family home; it weren't much anyway, just a leaky barrel. There never was no food and thar were ten of us sharing a barrel not big enough fer one. I thought it would be best if I made me way on me own. I walked the streets alone, me belly empty and aching and scratchin' me backbone, 'til I fell upon this 'House' and met me friends Brace and Tracy.

"Once they showed me the way here, and they took me in and did right by me. Without a cap ta me head or shoes ta me feet, they took me in and here I am. A warm place ta sleep, food for me belly, a clean, dry bed and they trained me ta work makin' shoes, all for ten cents a night.

"With all this good stuff, I got out on the street, not

pickin' rags no more, but a real job poundin' nails in the shoe factory. I have a home here, food in me belly and a job all because of this place. All far just ten cents a night.

"Now, boys, be good, use yar manners, be an ideal citizen like me and see what will become of ya."

Paddy stood on his perch, silent for a moment, and then lifted his head high and began to sing with a strong, clear voice ...

"We are home, we are home in love's warm embrace.
Our hearts are full of joy with a smile upon our face.
Though our troubles may be many and our toil long and hard,
We are home, we are home in love's warm embrace."

Slowly, all the boys joined together as they sang the verse again. Jack watched as the room grew silent and Paddy bowed slowly to his audience.

Suddenly a storm of applause, cat calls and hoots filled the room. With a grin on his face, Paddy leaped from the chair like a monkey and took another bow, soaking up the attention.

"That Paddy. He sure is a good one," said George with a sparkle in his eyes. "He speaks well, don't you think?"

Soon the back doors swung open, and Mary and Mrs. Tracy entered carrying huge bowls of apples. The boys cheered and passed the bowls around the room, munching on the crisp autumn fruit and filling their bellies again.

Jack had no sooner finished eating the core when Mr. Tracy stood and clapped his hands, and the room grew silent. The boys all stood and began forming lines. George pushed Jack and they filed out of the room.

"Where we going?"

"Time for bed," smiled George, poking him in the back to hurry along.

The boys marched past Mary and Mrs. Tracy as they bid the women good night with a smile or a nod. Mr. Tracy watched the boys, making sure they all minded their manners and acknowledged the ladies properly.

They climbed the staircase to the third floor, their steps echoing with pounding feet and tired chatter. The stairs opened into a great dormitory filled with row after row of bunk beds.

George grabbed Jack's hand and led him to an empty bunk at the end of the room. "My bed is over there, but I'll move down here with you so you won't be afraid."

"Afraid? I ain't afraid," snapped Jack.

Mr. Tracy soon found the two of them. "Thank you, George, for looking after our new lodger. I am sure you are getting to be fast chums. I just wanted you to know that you both will be among the children who will be going west by train to Michigan in a few days. You should get to know each other well, like brothers."

"Will my sister Sarah be going too? To Michigan? Riding the train with us all the way?" asked George eagerly. "I can't go unless Sarah goes." The young boy's bright blue eyes stared at Mr. Tracy.

"Yes, yes! There are families there that want daughters as well as sons in Michigan, and your sister will be going with us, too, as well as several other young ladies."

George's eyes lit up with the good news, and he wrapped his arms around Mr. Tracy's ample waist. "Oh, thank you, Mr. Tracy. Thank you.

"Did you hear that, Jack? We all will be finding new homes in Michigan and Sarah will be going with us, too." Jack nodded and smiled, uncertain if he really wanted to leave the Lodging House. Besides, he still didn't know what this place called Michigan was. He never had heard of it before; he only knew it was west.

"Mr. Tracy, if it is fine with you, I will bunk down here with Jack. I will make my bed and everything."

"No, George, tonight I think Jack might want to be down here by himself. I think he has some thinking to do. Is that right, Jack?"

Mr. Tracy helped Jack unroll his mattress and make up his bed with scratchy white sheets and a warm wool blanket.

Jack would not have minded if the boy had stayed near him, but with his belly so full and a warm, dry bed to enjoy for the first time in all the time he could remember, Jack knew sleep wasn't far off, and the boy was a talker.

George hung his head in disappointment. "Well, Jack, if ya need anything, I am just down the way. Jack, we're goin' ta Michigan ta find homes, and Sarah is gonna go with us. Ain't that somethin'?"

"G'night, Mr. Tracy. G'night, Jack," called George. They watched as the sandy-haired little boy made his way to his own bunk. He disappeared into a group of other boys as they all dressed down to their long johns and crawled into their squeaky bunk beds.

"He's a talker, that one," said Mr. Tracy. "Been here nearly six months; his sister is in the girls' hall. They have been orphaned nearly all their lives and living on the street until Mr. Brace brought them here. George is a good boy, and I hope you two become fast friends."

"Ya, he's a good kid, but I don't need ta be lookin' after a **wee** one. I hope ya know that."

"Jack, that wasn't why I wanted you to meet him. He's a good boy and he needs someone to look up to. I thought it would be good for the both of you. Keep an open mind, Jack. We all are here for a purpose, and the sooner you find yours, the better it will be for you."

Jack undressed to his long johns and crawled into the squeaky bunk with its cool sheets and warm blanket. His body was tired, his belly full and, for the first time, he wasn't scratching and digging at fleas and lice.

"Good night, Jack. I will see you in the morning."

Jack watched as Mr. Tracy made his rounds to the rows of bunks. He was chatting with the boys, pulling covers over some, moving boots out of the aisle, and tidying up the spaces. Slowly all over the room, the oil lamps were dampered and the room grew dark.

Chapter Eight
All Aboard!
Thursday, September 28, 1854

The next nine days at the Lodging House passed
quickly for Jack. Each morning, he and the other boys
arose early to hot water and clean towels in the
washroom. They ate a breakfast of **gruel** and buttermilk
before going to the classroom where they learned to
recite the alphabet, write their names and **cipher**
numbers. Jack felt the brains in his skull grow and fill
with interesting facts and ideas. He came up with
thoughts he never had had before and possibilities that
made him want to learn more.

After their midday meal, Jack and other boys learned
the art of shoe making so they could find work in the
nearby shoe factory, if necessary. Vocations were
important for boys, especially for those who were too
old to be placed-out. Learning a skill would give them
an opportunity to make money, move from the Lodging
House and eventually move into a boarding house to
live on their own.

The collection of wages, saved for the boys in a bank,
was thought only to be something for the rich.
However, Mr. Tracy provided a box where they could

deposit their money in their own names to be kept for them until it was needed. The money never was touched by anyone except its owner, and Mr. Tracy was an honorable man.

The Lodging House was a good place for Jack. He soon made many friends and met other boys with whom he would travel west to find homes.

There were Dick and Seth, who said they had slept in nearly all the station houses in the city. They were real snoozers and made friends with everyone they met.

There was Taylor, who when he first arrived at the Lodging House and was informed of the trip to Michigan, was happier than anyone else to go; he always had wanted to travel on a train. When given his traveling clothes, Taylor was fitted with a pair of boots, something he said he hadn't had as a cover for his feet in three winters.

There also was Liverpool, who had been named after the city of his birth and, luckily, had been found at the Five Points just hours before departure. Liverpool had been orphaned and homeless in England before coming to America. He made his living on the docks of New York City by running errands and doing odd jobs for the sailors. He dressed in **castoff** clothes and when he bathed at the Lodging House, it was said he had so many pieces of torn clothes wrapped and tied around him that he looked like a walking rag bundle.

Liverpool was cleaned, **deloused**, given a haircut, a suit of clothes and boots and then taken to the docks just in time to board the steamer *Isaac Newton* along with the other thirty-seven boys and girls who were in search of new homes in that faraway place called Michigan.

All was a jumble of excitement at the docks as **hampers** of food and bundles of blankets were removed from the wagon along with the boys and girls, ages six to fifteen. The children lined up in the cool autumn evening waiting to load aboard the **steamship** for their trip up the Hudson River from Manhattan to Albany. The river itself was busy; filled with ships of all kinds— **schooners**, **barges** and **yachts**.

It was there, waiting for the boat, that the Supervising Agent for the trip, Rev. Edwin P. Smith, reintroduced himself to the children.

Jack smiled as the introductions were made. In less then two weeks at the Lodging House, he had became a different person; he wondered if Mr. Smith would recognize him in his new blue uniform and white shirt.

As Jack waited, Edwin made announcements concerning their trip.

"Boys and girls, please gather around," he called them to attention. "I am your supervisor, Edwin, and I expect you all to address me by my formal name and use respect with me at all times.

"Some of you I have met." Smith glanced over to Jack and nodded to him. Jack smiled back proudly.

"And still, there are others of you that I am meeting for the very first time.

"We are about to embark upon a great adventure together. An adventure that will change the course of your young lives and give you opportunities that you never would have thought possible. As you know, we are westward bound, traveling first by water on this side-wheeler by the name of *Isaac Newton*."

Mr. Smith held out a long arm and gestured across the dock. The children's eyes followed as they turned to look at the ship with its peeling white paint and flat, open decks that were loaded with crates and bundles. Jack wasn't sure if it looked safe.

"The *Isaac Newton* will take us to a place called

Albany," continued Smith. "Some of you might have heard of this city before. It is a place still within the state of New York. At Albany, we then will board a rail car to Buffalo."

"A train!" interrupted Taylor in delight. "We will be riding a train!"

"Yes, son, we will be riding on two trains during our travels," added Mr. Smith.

Taylor clapped his hands loudly. "Two trains—just think of it."

Smith continued. "In Buffalo, we will board another boat that will take us over one of the largest lakes you ever will see. That lake's name is Lake Erie. The passage on that boat will take us to our first location in the state of Michigan to the city called Detroit.

"From Detroit, we will board the Michigan Central Rail Road; a train line that graciously has arranged for us to have free transportation across the entire state. This train will take all of you, boys and girls, to your new homes.

"None of us, including myself, ever have been to this state called Michigan, but I am told it is rich and green and that the people are generous and ready to make homes for all of you.

"We must work together. We must cooperate with one another and be kind. You older children are asked to please help with the younger ones. If we all work together, we will have a peaceful and happy trip to your new homes.

"I want to warn any of you who are thinking of being rascals on this trip. This is not the place nor the time for you to misbehave or cause problems. Any of you not fully participating, not fully using your manners, or not fully obeying all of my requests will be sent immediately back to the Lodging House here in New York City. Never again will you have an opportunity to embark on such an adventure with the Children's Aid Society.

"Now, is that understood?"

All the children from George, the youngest, to the very oldest boys and girls at fifteen, nodded their heads in agreement. They knew this was the first and possibly last opportunity for them to find homes off the streets of the city.

Jack watched as George, who had become like a little brother, now clung onto his sister, Sarah, who was only a couple years older. He held her hand and leaned happily against her wanting to be as close as he could be. Jack knew he would have to help them both.

The children milled around, waiting, trying to stay out of the way of the fancy-dressed passengers who passed by them on the docks. These passengers moved up the **gangplank** loading their baggage aboard the *Isaac Newton* into small rooms above the main level.

The great hoopskirts of the women danced in the breezes as they walked delicately up the planks being helped by their gentlemanly escorts who took their hands and guided them safely aboard.

Mr. Smith was busy arranging their supplies when a wagon pulled up carrying Mr. Brace, Mr. and Mrs. Tracy, and Mary. Mary sat in the back of the wagon and carried a large basket filled with apples.

Mr. Brace and Mr. Tracy helped the women down from the wagon and carried the basket to the waiting children.

The children cheered with excitement when they spied their friends and the food.

"We thought we would come to see you off on your great adventure," said Mr. Brace as Mary and Mr. and Mrs. Tracy passed out the apples.

"We wish you all well," said Mrs. Tracy. Jack could see tears in her eyes. Mary was too busy with the apples, and too tough, to shed any tears.

Sarah pulled loose from George and wrapped her arms around Mrs. Tracy's waist and hugged her tightly. "Remember me?" asked Sarah as she pushed back her bonnet and smiled up at Mrs. Tracy.

"How should I ever forget you, dear?" replied Mrs. Tracy, hugging her back.

"Now, children," called Mr. Tracy. "Children, please come together. Let us hear you sing one last song. Does anyone have a song to share? Please, sing out with a clear, loud voice for everyone to hear."

Jack quickly remembered the song he had heard the first night upon arriving at the Lodging House. He had sung it many times since with Paddy. Paddy, unfortunately, wasn't along with them on the trip as he had been placed-out just days before having found a home in upstate New York. He was missed by all the children, including Jack.

Jack cleared his throat and led the chorus of the song.

"We are home, we are home in love's
warm embrace ..."

The children's voices joined together loudly as passengers aboard the *Isaac Newton* stuck their heads out of their staterooms and others gathered on the deck to listen.

"Our hearts are full of joy with a smile upon
our face.
Though our troubles may be many and our toil
long and hard,
We are home, we are home in love's warm embrace."

64

When the children finished, the passengers applauded and the Tracys sadly wished the children well as they hugged them all. Even Mary now dabbed tears from her eyes as she pulled the children to her and gave them great, loving hugs.

Charles Loring Brace shook hands with Rev. Edwin P. Smith. Then the captain rang the boarding bell, for it was time for their adventure to begin. It was time for them to find homes.

Chapter Nine
The Great Adventure

One by one, the children filed aboard waving good-bye to Mr. Brace, the Tracys, and Mary. Mr. Smith counted to make sure that all thirty-seven children were in the group.

The great double smoke stacks of the *Isaac Newton* belched smelly, black clouds into the air. The pulsing motion of the side-wheeler, as its paddles scooped at the water, could be felt by all as the ship bumped clumsily against the wooden pier and moved away from the dock.

Since the steamboat company would not provide free passage to help the children find new homes, the only accommodations Mr. Brace could secure for the children were **emigrant** or **steerage**. These were the cheapest tickets available. The children had to sit and sleep on the floor of the ship's lowest level on rough, stinking mats. The mats had been chewed by rats and were saturated with the smell of urine and vomit.

Since most of the children had never traveled by boat before, they were afraid. They huddled together under their blankets and hoped the trip to Albany would be over quickly.

They had just settled into their stinking quarters with

Mr. Smith, who was trying his best to comfort them, when a voice called out from the stairwell.

"Mr. Smith, sir, are you here with the children?"

Making his way carefully forward, trying not to step on fingers and feet in the semi-darkness, Smith found his way to the low-hanging steps.

"Mr. Smith, sir?" said a low voice. "The captain has sent me down here to invite you and the children above deck to his salon to have a meal and perhaps listen to the children sing once again, if that would be possible."

"Well, the children are all settled in now, and I would hate to disturb them."

"Mr. Smith, sir, the captain feels bad that the children have to stay down below here when there are open **berths** above that have not been sold. He thought perhaps, for the price of the children's company and a song, he might be able to make arrangements ... "

"Yes, of course we could come to the captain's quarters. Children, children ... "

Smith quickly helped everyone to their feet, and Jack made himself useful by making sure that George and his sister were together and safe. They folded their blankets and packed them away. They straightened their hair, buttoned their jackets, and followed the man on the stairs up to the captain's salon.

The salon was large and filled with a table heaped with fresh fruits and vegetables, cold meats, cheeses, and white and brown bread.

"It is a shame that you children have to sleep in such deplorable conditions," said the captain addressing the group. "I myself have children and would never want them to sleep in steerage. It seems that the rich men of this fine city could have seen to the needs of you children to find proper boarding aboard my vessel. But since they did not, it is up to me to provide this," stated the captain.

"Children, please help yourself to the food and, afterward, perhaps you will share with me one of your lovely songs. Like the one I heard you sing earlier. After that, I'm sure we will be able to find proper bunks for you all to sleep in."

Grateful for the generosity, the children filled
their stomachs, and when finished, sang a song of
thanksgiving to show their appreciation.

"Splendid, splendid ... children, you have the voices
of angels. I want you to know that I myself also was an
orphan and lived many years alone. I wandered the
streets until I was taken in by a kindly old sea captain
who taught me the ways of the water and here I am
today, a captain myself, because of my kindly
benefactor.

"You all will make something of yourselves with
the help of kindly people and the hearing of kind words.
And don't ever forget the importance of a good
education ... Look to your future and believe there is
something good there waiting for you as there was
for me."

Jack listened and hoped the captain's words would
come true for him, too. He already had learned more in
just the short time he had stayed at the Lodging House
than he had been taught in nearly his whole life. His
Mum would be so proud of him, and his Da would not
have believed it would have been possible.

That night, the boys and girls separated and slept in
vacant staterooms in warm bunks with soft blankets on
opposite sides of the ship.

The next morning the children numbered only
thirty-five because during Mr. Smith's evening **vigil**, as
he watched over the children, he was approached by two
sets of passengers who each wanted to take one of the
boys. One boy was to be placed in a home in Rochester,
New York, and the other boy, Liverpool, was to go live
with a merchant along the Mississippi River in the state
of Illinois; another place none of the children had ever
heard of before.

The **side-wheeler**, *Isaac Newton*, arrived as scheduled in Albany at six in the morning, and the children said their good-byes to the boys who already had found new homes.

Liverpool could not believe his luck. He had thought he was the least likely to have found a home as he had had no education from the Lodging House and had yet to acquire his manners.

It gave all the children hope that homes would be waiting for them too in this faraway place called Michigan.

Mr. Smith, along with Jack and the older boys, worked to unload their traveling supplies. The older girls kept a watchful eye on the younger children who sat dangling their feet over the dock as they watched the boats enter and leave the harbor.

The train they were to meet would not leave until noon. Over the next few hours, the children ate sour pickles and cheese, munched on dried bread and shared sweet cider from a jug.

Smith watched as the children chased each other up and down the docks. The girls braided each other's hair, and the boys flipped marbles back and forth to one another.

Jack was amazed as he watched all the boats that left and arrived. Many passengers, speaking weird and different languages, crowded around waiting for the next ship or wagon that would take them closer to their homes.

Jack checked his pocket and found his five matches were still there. Matches left from his past life; matches that would remind him not to look back but to move forward with the help of the Children's Aid Society and Mr. Smith.

Chapter Ten
Room for One More
Friday, September 29, 1854

Sitting on a large wooden box on the dock, Jack squinted in the morning sun as he watched George and Sarah talking quietly and playing with a long string of yellow yarn. Jack smiled at the two of them; he was happy for George that he and his sister were together again.

Mr. Smith had completed all his tasks and he, too, sat lazily in the sun with the children waiting for their train to arrive.

Jack moved around on his perch and swung his feet back and forth gently bumping the crate and keeping time as he sang, "We are home, we are home ... " softly to himself, when from beneath him he felt a sharp blow.

Startled, Jack jumped to his feet as the crate mysterious moved by itself and lifted up off the dock. Two dirty, bare feet appeared from beneath.

Slowly the crate tumbled over sideways, and there stood a dirty-faced boy with tangled hair that was matted to the side of his head. He wore a patched coat and pants so big that they hung low on his hips and were tied to him with a rope.

"Hey, what's up? Ya trying ta scare the bejeezers out of me or something? I was just sleeping nice and peaceful like, and here you are all dressed in your fancy duds, poundin' on me house and wakin' me from my sleep. A man needs his sleep don't ya know? Or are you a **dandy** who doesn't have ta work and yous don't mind buggin' a workin' man?"

Jack grinned at the boy, recognizing the speech and slang of a fellow **snoozer**.

"So what's yar excuse, kid? Ya just lookin' fer trouble?"

"No, no trouble from me."

"Yea, of course not. No trouble ever. You and your fancy clothes. Ya probably have a rich father and a fat mother who bakes lots of pies and cakes for ya ta eat. Ya probably never slept a night outside with the dogs and pigs a day in yar life. Have ya?"

Jack didn't know what to say. He never had been mistaken for a person of **substance** before. He never had been mistaken for anything other than a thief.

The boy was smelly and dirty and pushed up against Jack. "You have money, kid?" he asked in a low, threatening tone.

Just then, the boy flew sidewise through the air and flopped onto the dock. It was George, falling upon him with tooth and nail. He dove at the snoozer in rage and began pounding him with his small fists. The boy howled in pain and grabbed George by the hair, trying to pull him off.

Jack jumped into the scramble and yanked George from atop the boy shaking him from his momentary madness.

"Leave him alone, you bully!" shouted George. "Leave my friend alone!"

The boy jumped to his feet and turned to take off

74

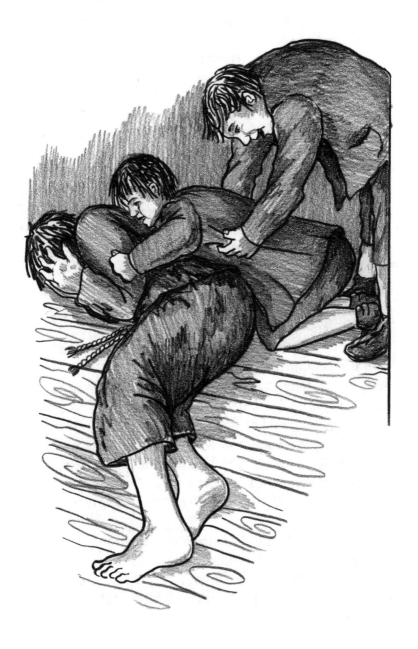

when Sarah, not one to be left out, stepped in front of him and tripped the boy, knocking him down again.

Hearing the commotion, Smith ran to the circle of children who began to form as they pinned the snoozer to the rough boards of the dock and held him there.

"What you do to one, you do to us all!" shouted George, standing over the boy and daring him to say something.

"Stop! Stop!" Jack shouted. "He didn't do anything. He's a bummer, a snoozer, like us."

"What's going on?" demanded Smith as he broke through the ring of children and stared down at the boy who was being bullied and badgered by the young travelers.

"He tried to beat on Jack," cried George as he burst into angry tears.

"He tried to beat on my brother," chimed in Sarah as she reached out and pulled George to her as both of them cried.

The other children agreed. "That's what happened. We seen it with our own eyes."

Mr. Smith looked at Jack and scowled. "Eat 'em up Jack, are you at the bottom of this?"

The boy who lay flat on the dock rose slowly to his feet, hoping to escape before the attention was turned to him again, but the circle of children shouldered close together and wouldn't let him go.

"And who do we have here?" questioned Smith as he turned to the boy.

The boy stood mute in fear before the group.

"Answer the man," snapped Jack.

"I'm John. My name is John, but everyone calls me Smack 'cause that's all they do to me, just gives me a smack."

"Where do you live, John? Where are your parents?"

76

"I don't live nowhere and I ain't got no parents. I live in that box."

"I see," said Smith as he looked around, ashamed of the children who were picking on someone who was in the same condition as the rest of them had been just weeks and months before.

"John ... my name is Rev. Smith, and I am from the Children's Aid Society of New York City. These children you see before you also are orphans and half-orphans. They all have lived on the streets with no place to call their home and with no one to look after them. They are just like you."

"Yea, well, they look like someone looks after them now. Look and see all their fancy duds, scrubbed clean and lookin' like they have money ta spare, jingling in their pockets."

"Jack here, your new friend, has only had a home with us for a little over a week. We all are on our way to Michigan to find homes. Would you like to accompany us and find yourself a home?"

John's dirty face scrunched up against the morning sun as he looked at Smith. He had no idea if this man was trying to trick him or not.

"Who will speak for this boy?" Smith asked the children. He was ashamed of their actions and was trying to teach them a lesson in charity.

"Do you know him or someone who was like him once? Who can recommend this boy as someone suitable to belong to our company?"

Smith knew the children knew nothing of this boy, only that he was as hard up as any of them. He had no father or mother or anyone to live with. He slept his nights away, shivering alone in his crate.

"We are going to Michigan, son, to make farmers out of these boys and girls and to live in the country. Would you like to do that?"

John slowly nodded his head yes. He had watched and met many people along the docks who were visiting from the country. He had watched as apples and peaches were unloaded from the boats and as crates of vegetables arrived for the markets. Yes, he would like to live in the country with all that food so he always would have plenty to eat even if he had no money to buy it with.

"Yes, I would like to be a farmer and live in the country," stammered John.

"Who will speak for this boy?"

Jack stood forward and looked up at Mr. Smith, remembering what it was like to be hungry without enough food and freezing in the winter. "I say we take 'im with us. What ya say?"

The crowd was silent with their eyes staring down at their feet, ashamed by their lack of manners and how easily they had forgotten where they came from.

"George?" questioned Jack. "What do ya say?"

George hid his face behind his sister's shoulder, and when he looked up at Jack, tears fell from his eyes.

"Sure, what's one more?"

"But he is dirty and smells bad," remarked one of the older girls.

"He can wash and we will find clothes for him," commented Mr. Smith, assuring the girl.

"He is one of us. He needs ta come along," said Jack, and the group of children softly agreed.

"We will have to squeeze together even more than we are now and our purse is scant, but we will make do. So, are we in agreement?"

The children nodded their heads as they made room for one more, who, just moments before, they were ready to throw into the harbor.

Smith stared down at the filthy boy whose blue eyes looked tired and weary. He knew it would be difficult to find him a home, as it would be with the others. But perhaps he would do well; at any rate, he must try. If left alone to float here a few more months in the winter cold, the boy's end was certain.

Smith left the group in the charge of the older children and led John back to the *Isaac Newton* where he met privately with the captain and pleaded the boy's case. He needed a place for the boy to be scrubbed clean and, if possible, find him a suit of clothes and boots.

The kindly captain listened and agreed to help rescue the child, preparing him to find a new home in the country and away from the dangers of the docks.

After a hard scrubbing, delousing and a haircut performed by the captain himself, John was presented with an old blue suit and a white shirt that once belonged to a cabin boy who had lost his life along the river months before. The suit, though not a perfect fit, was clean and neat and were the best clothes John ever had worn. The only thing not available was a pair of boots as the cabin boy had taken them with him to the bottom of the river.

"That is alright with me," said John, delighted with his clothes. "I ain't never really had meself a pair of boots anyway. I was born barefoot, so they told me, and I guess I'll be staying that-a-way."

Mr. Smith and the captain smiled at the boy and were happy to see his hopeful spirit. Before Smith left, the captain reached into his pocket and pulled out a five dollar piece.

"This is to help with the children's needs," he said, "or perhaps you can find that boy a pair of boots." Smith shook hands with the captain who waved good-bye to John.

That afternoon Rev. Smith entered into his record book, "John – American – Protestant - 13 years old – Orphan – Parents died in Maine- A 'snoozer' for four years – Most of the time in New York City with an occasional visit to Albany and Troy, 'when times got hard' – Intelligent – Black, sharp eyes – Hopeful."

Chapter Eleven
All Aboard! Again!

As the time grew near noon, the children, including John, marched together, two by two, to the train depot. Rev. Smith counted thirty-six children to make sure they all were together.

As they passed down the dock and through the crowds of people, many times John's old name was called from gangs of children who gathered around.

"Smack, is that you? Are ya being shanghaied?"

"Smack, are ya in need of help?"

"Hey, look! Smack is a dandy!"

John smiled and waved good-bye to his street pals. He was glad to be leaving them and all they represented behind.

At the train station, Mr. Smith was stopped by a man in a blue uniform from the train company.

"Rev. E. P. Smith? Rev. E. P. Smith, sir?" he called in a somber way.

"Yes. I am E. P. Smith. May I help you?"

"Sir, I believe these belong to you."

When his name was called, Smith and all the children turned to look at the man in the blue uniform. Behind him were nine more orphans who had been sent from

New York City by the Children's Aid Society to join the group. The man handed Mr. Smith a letter which he immediately opened and read.

Jack watched as a worried look came over Smith's face. Nine more children now were added to their party and made their number forty-five. Introductions were made all around, and the new children were welcomed.

Together, they made their way through the crowds of people at the train station where voices in many different languages and accents called out to loved ones; the noise filled the air. The voices of Germans, Irish, Italians, French, and Norwegians cried out in confusion looking for their baggage, looking for the right train car, looking for the right city. All was confusion and babel, and the air was heavy with fear and anger.

"Dis America is a bad place to be," cried one.

"It's better I starve in the old country," howled another.

"I wish I never had left home," cried still another.

The children huddled together, holding hands and staying as close as they could without walking on one another.

John cried out, over and over, as travelers, emigrants and porters stomped on his bare feet and moved on without notice.

Taylor's dark eyes stared at the train in amazement. He couldn't wait to board.

"Children, stay here. I must check with the conductor to secure our train car and passage. Do not move. Do not leave this area. Above all, everyone watch over the one beside you. Do you understand?"

The children drew close for safety and agreed to stay in one place until Smith returned. They watched as he wove his way along the platform to talk to a red-faced, round man in a uniform who carried a whistle between his teeth.

The children paid close attention, especially the girls, not taking their eyes off Mr. Smith until he lifted his hand high in the air and signaled for them to hurry and join him. At that, the children grabbed their partners and dodged along the platform toward a large train car that stood waiting.

A man in a uniform turned and opened the giant sliding door of the car. As soon as he placed a stool down for the children to enter, they were swamped by emigrants grabbing their bags and cases and pushing the children out of the way.

"Hurry, children! Hurry!" cried Mr. Smith as he tried to jam aboard the train bundles of blankets and hampers of food that had been delivered to the depot by wagon from the boat.

Smith was pushed and shoved in every direction until the older boys lent a hand and pushed back. Finally, he was able to load all their belongings aboard.

Jack reached for George and Sarah. He held on tightly to both of them and helped them up into the train car. John cried out in pain over and over, jumping and hopping about trying to protect his feet. Taylor pushed them all from behind, only wanting to board and not be left behind.

The swarm of humanity, smelling of sweat and garlic, forced their way into the car along with the children.

"No! No!" cried Smith. "This car is reserved for the children ONLY. You must leave!"

Angry words in every accent were shouted into the air at Mr. Smith and, as soon as the car was jammed to overflowing, an iron bar slammed across the opening and the giant door was pulled partway shut.

"Children! Children, are you all here? Push your way

to the back of the car if you can."

Voices called out to Mr. Smith in every direction, assuring him all were aboard.

One by one and two by two, the children pushed themselves through the crowd, using the street smarts they had learned long ago. They made their way over the benches and around the bags and luggage to the safety of Mr. Smith until all forty-five children were together.

Because there were no windows, the car was semi-dark. It was filled with the stink of too many people who were almost suffocating from the closeness of each other. Some people stood because there wasn't room for all to sit. Others sat on laps, and still others huddled on the floor under or near the benches.

The benches of rough wood had no backs, but it didn't matter since there were so many people. Everyone was all sealed together shoulder to shoulder, hip to hip, with no place to move and no chance of moving except together.

Soon a great bell clanged. They could feel the rumble and the movement of the wheels beneath them. The air grew sickening sweet with the smell of dirty bodies. An Irishman with a think accent swore loudly and threw open the side door. He hung out his head, loosing his stomach in the rushing air that was filled with flying sparks from the smokestack of the train's engine.

The air filled the car and blew the travelers' hair and scarves in every direction. Caps flew and babies cried out.

Mr. Smith pulled George and Sarah from the open door in fear they would be sucked out with the great rush of wind. It would be a long, cramped trip as the train chugged westward. When night came on, the large door was pulled partly closed again, enveloping them all in near darkness.

Lanterns that hung from hooks on the wall were removed and lit. The children looked around and found their lamp, but Mr. Smith had no matches. Jack reached into his pocked and felt the five matches he had kept, just in case, and realized he would have to forfeit one of them now for the betterment of all. Five matches for a nickel meal. With only four, he would have to beg for the other penny. He had begged many times and could do it again if necessary.

Jack nudged Mr. Smith and gave him a match. Smith looked up at Jack, remembering the first time he had met this lumber merchant, and smiled.

"Thank you, Jack. This is a big help. I am glad you and your matches are along."

Jack pushed his red hair out of his eyes and smiled at Mr. Smith with pride.

The children crowded around the lamp, putting out their hands, hoping to protect the fragile flame. Smith struck the match to his boot heel and quickly touched it to the wick inside the tin chamber. When the wick lit, Smith carefully shut the lantern door and latched it closed, placing it securely back on its hook.

The children all cheered. The dim light of the lantern was just enough for them to see Mr. Smith at all times and to let them know they were safe.

As Jack watched, he could see the other passengers passing bottles of alcohol among themselves. He also heard their bad jokes and bawdy songs. Mr. Smith, also aware of the jokes and songs, tried to keep the children together and occupy their minds and ears, protecting them from this unruly group of travelers. Song after song was sung softly by the children. Soon snores and grunts filled the air, and the lanterns were extinguished around the car.

Mr. Smith distributed the blankets, and the children drew together to comfort one another and endure the darkness.

The train car was hot and, along with the stink of human flesh, it was nearly impossible for them to sleep. Here and there around the train car, another pipe was lit and more smoke was added to the thick air.

An old man, who sat in the midst of the children and spoke only German, decided he would have a pipe and sat puffing away. The substance he smoked in the pipe smelled like urine-soaked hay from a horse barn. The puffs of stink filled the air and made even Mr. Smith choke and cough.

"Excuse me, sir. Would you mind putting your pipe out as it might make the children sick?" Mr. Smith asked politely.

Jack watched as the man ignored Mr. Smith and kept on puffing away at his stinky bowl.

"Please," pleaded Mr. Smith. "For the sake of the children and the other travelers."

The man with his big, bushy eyebrows lifted them and tilted his head in Smith's direction. He puffed even harder, making a smudge of the air and throwing Smith into a coughing fit.

It was hopeless, and the children watched as the old man smugly settled into his seat and began to sway back and forth with the rolling and rumbling of the car. He puffed away contently, leaving Mr. Smith with nothing to do but sit down.

Jack continued to stare at the old man and wondered if he hadn't understood the request. But someplace in Jack's heart, he knew this was just the old man's way, and he didn't care if anyone liked it or not.

Soon the old man leaned back in his seat and appeared to be falling asleep. The curls of smoke drifted

from the bowl of his pipe and added to the smoky haze that filled the car. Jack, feeling drowsy himself, closed his eyes for a moment when—"Smash!"—something flew threw through the air past him and slammed into the wall of the car.

Startled, Jack straightened up and opened his eyes just in time to see tiny, glowing embers floating in the air. Lying in the shadows in a pile on the floor was the old man's pipe which was broken into a million pieces where it had hit the wall of the train car.

The old man jumped to his feet and shouted out in his native tongue at the children around him, pointing his finger and raising his fist. Smith quickly jumped to his feet to let the old man know that no harm was to come to the children and he had better settle down.

An older woman sitting near them chuckled and clapped her hands as the old man howled in anger. He pushed his way out of the group of children and shoved his way to the front of the car, tripping over people as he went.

Jack looked and saw John sitting directly behind the seat where the old man had sat. As the shadows played upon John's face, Jack could see his smug and satisfied look.

The night train rolled on until it pulled into the station at Utica, New York, where most of the travelers departed, including the grouchy old man who no longer had his pipe. With so many getting off the train, there now was more room for everyone. The children spread out onto the benches and the floor. Soon they fell into a restless slumber as the car swayed back and forth.

By morning the train had made it to Rochester. Jack rubbed the sleep from his eyes and, leaning on one elbow, looked about him. The passengers were just starting to wake up. Some yawned, some groaned, and nearly all spit. The women opened their bundles of bread and cheese to fed their hungry families, and they wiped the bottoms of dirty babies. A bucket was placed in the back of the car for those who needed to relieve themselves. The stench rose and filled the air. Mr. Smith crawled over the benches and the children. He pulled the sliding door open again, allowing the air to circulate and clean the stink from the car.

Jack reached back and poked John to wake him up, and the action was repeated over and over until all the children were aroused. Smith drew the hamper of food from beneath his bench and passed out apples and pears to the children along with dry bread. A kindly old woman, who carried a **basket-bottle** of water, offered to share it with the children. She spoke no English but understood the children were traveling alone with Mr. Smith and were in need. She grinned a wrinkly, toothless smile as she made her rounds with the bottle offering them just enough to help them swallow their bread and then pulling it from their lips.

Mr. Smith was grateful for the woman's generosity, as he had not thought to bring along a basket-bottle for the children. Something he would not forget again.

After they ate, they took turns watching out the opened door of the train car as they quickly passed through the countryside.

The questions soon flew through the air as the children shouted out inquiries about the country life. Mr. Smith, for the first time, realized that none of them ever had seen miles of green trees and grass or farm fields and pastures of cattle.

Smith joined the children standing at the door, holding on to the steel rod that secured them from the wind.

"What's that, Mister?" asked John.

89

"A cornfield," replied Smith. "Corn is good and filling. You can eat it on the cob, boil it into gruel, make it into cakes ... "

"Yea, I've begged corn cakes before."

When they roared through orchards that were loaded with big, red harvest apples, it was hard to keep the children from tumbling off the train. Their hands reached out stretching for the lovely red fruit still hanging on the trees.

"Oh, just look at 'em. Growing right off the tree. Ain't seen nothin' like that before."

Jack couldn't keep the smile from his face. If so much food also grew in this place called Michigan, he never would leave.

Soon excitement again filled the air as the children's voices rang out with joy. Outside, just beyond the whirling wind, was a large harvested cornfield which now was spread over with bright orange pumpkins.

"Look at 'em all growing."

"Just look at 'em," echoed through the car. George grabbed his sister and yanked her to her feet. They looked out the door in amazement.

The toothless old woman who shared her water also stood and stared. A crooked finger pointed out and shook in the air as she stuttered words in broken English. "Be-u-tee-ful! Good to eat!"

"Ah, fellers," John piped up. "Ain't that great country—won't we have wondrous things ta eat? Oh! Oh! Just look at 'em! If there be such wonders in Michigan, then I am all for that place. Three cheers for Michigan!"

Jack agreed and cheered with the rest, wishing he were already there.

The train rolled through the countryside filling the children with awe and wonder.

Soon the train began to slow, and all the passengers around them began to organize their belongings and adjust their clothes. The next stop was Buffalo.

Chapter Twelve
Across Lake Erie
Saturday, September 30, 1854

Jack helped George and Sarah fold their blankets and pull their things together. Mr. Smith checked the food hamper and snapped it closed. All the children were tired, restless and wished their travels were over, but they knew Michigan was still a long way off.

Jack watched as some of the older girls helped the children straighten their hair. They dusted off the dirt that had gathered on their clothes from sleeping on the floor under the benches.

Sarah brushed dust from George's uniform, and George pulled a piece of straw from Sarah's hair.

As Jack buttoned his jacket, he received a sharp jab to his side from John. In his hands he held the broken pieces of the old man's pipe. Picking up the stem and jamming it into his mouth, he crossed his arms over his chest puffing away and scowling like the old man. Both boys burst out in laughter as the stem fell from John's mouth and rolled on the dirty floor under the benches.

At Buffalo, the children followed Mr. Smith as if he were the Pied Piper as he led them from the train to the boat docks of Lake Erie. Here, they all were introduced to Mr. Harrison and Mr. Noble who were to help them in their travels.

Mr. Harrison was a **freight agent** for the boat they were about to board. He was expecting the children and hoped to make their nine-hour stay at the docks a pleasant one. He already had accepted and was looking after their bundles of blankets and hampers of food that had been taken off a wagon sent from the train station.

Mr. Noble was an agent from the Michigan Central Rail Road. He gave a letter of introduction to Mr. Smith that would help the group as they traveled by train from Detroit to their final destination in Dowagiac.

During their wait at the docks, the children strolled by the large passenger ships. They played on the crates and boxes that were waiting to be loaded, teased stray dogs and patted the heads of the great horses that pulled the freight wagons.

Jack occupied himself with an ugly, three-legged mutt that snarled and chased after the children. It reminded him of the dog at Five Points that had befriended him and saved him many times from tough guys and the Metropolitans. Jack wondered if he ever would have a dog of his very own, something he always had wanted.

Soon Mr. Harrison and Mr. Smith called everyone together. Mr. Smith counted as Mr. Harrison led the group up the gangplank, two by two, onto the ship and down sharp steps to a level below the waterline and into steerage.

It was better, they thought, than the side-wheeler on the Hudson; at least this place had berths covered with coarse horsehair mattresses. However, they soon discovered that it would have been better if they had slept on the floor because the mattresses crawled with bedbugs and hopped with fleas. Few of the mattresses ever had been changed or cleaned, and personal vermin left behind by the last passengers was there waiting for the children.

Not wanting to sleep on the filthy berths, the children stood around and sat on the wooden benches. But they soon realized that if they didn't want a bed to sleep in, there were many other emigrants who would be happy to push them aside and crawl in.

Soon, steerage was filled with a mass of people speaking every known language and accent. "America truly was made up of people from all over the world," thought Jack, as he tried to settle into a repeat of the night before on the train.

Mr. Smith tried his best to advise the children as he handed out the blankets. "Never mind the bedbugs and just try to get a good night's sleep. You will need it for the coming days."

Jack reluctantly crawled up into a low, stinky berth that smelled like seasickness. He covered his nose and buried his head in the blanket trying not to breathe too deeply. No sooner had he settled in when he was pushed over, and up hopped John beside him.

"Move over. Don't pig the bed. Ain't nothin' like sleepin' on a mattress, don't ya think?"

Jack thought back to remember that just a few weeks earlier he would have felt the same way. Now, as he felt the occasional nip of a bedbug and the spring of a flea, he felt dirty.

Throughout steerage, the lanterns stayed lit during the night, while hazy smoke filled the room from the stinking pipes of old men. Jack and John peeked out from their bunk and watched as emigrant travelers spent the night talking, rinsing out dirty diapers, smoking, playing dice and singing.

From above them came stamping sounds of horses' hooves along with the bleating of sheep and the clucking of chickens. The farm animals were shipped one floor above them. Occasionally the ceiling oozed with a shower of urine that washed through the cracks and fell down upon the motley travelers.

The children all were glad to know that by tomorrow night they would be in port at Detroit. They hoped they never would again have to spend another night in such filth and torment.

As the first light of morning shown through the stairwell, the children, who hardly had slept because of seasickness and the endless bites of bedbugs and fleas, made their way through the piles of people and luggage to the upper deck for some fresh air and sunshine.

There, the cold breeze blew the stink from their clothes and gave them hope again that the trip soon would be over. The great Lake Erie spread before them. The water shimmered in the morning sun and looked as if a million sparkles danced upon it. Jack remembered how the water at the docks in New York City had shimmered the same way just like the clean halls of the Lodging House.

Groups of children gathered on the deck as they groomed one another, straightening hair, picking fleas and bugs, and dusting off their clothes. During the day, they ate their meal on deck and talked with other passengers. One group of men traveling together was on their way back to Michigan where they lived. They were three brothers who had a farm near the center of the state in a place called Lansing. They said it had been declared the state's capital only seven years earlier in 1847.

Mr. Smith and the children gathered around to hear tales of the new state they would call home.

"The woods are so deep and thick ya'd get lost in an instant if ya aren't careful, so ya better all stick close to

96

Mr. Smith and listen to what he tells ya," said one brother with a wide, joking smile.

"And the skeeters are as big as birds, and they will darn near carry ya away, especially if yar'e small, like this little one," said the short brother pointing to George.

"What's a skeeter?" questioned George in horror.

"It is a wild, biting bug that will suck yar blood away and leave ya all covered with welts and sores. Sometimes, when it's really bad, it will leave ya with a fever, shaking all over so ya can't even work or eat."

"I always can eat," joked Jack, and the children and men laughed.

"What about the native people, the Indians? Are they still around?" asked John.

"Yes, ya'll see them come to town or market with their wives and children. They mostly keep ta themselves and grow their corn and make maple syrup ta sell. Ya know all the land of Michigan once belonged ta those people."

The children all stood wide-eyed and listened. "Michigan sounded like a wondrous place," thought Jack.

"Do ya know what a bear is?" asked the tallest of the brothers.

None of the children responded until John stood forward. "I know bears. I saw one on a chain outside the wagon of a **tinker man** once. They are great, hairy beasts with long claws and sharp teeth."

"You got it, boy. That's the ones. They live in Michigan and roam the woods. Fierce they are but good for the eatin'."

The children laughed and hoped the men were joking.

"Hey, I knows a song of Michigan. Would ya'll like ta

learn it for the keepin' and I won't charge ya a cent?"

"Too bad Paddy isn't with us. He'd sing it right back to ya," commented George, and the children all chimed in, agreeing with George.

Mr. Smith smiled as he watched the brothers, all who were younger than himself, prepare to present the song. It was obvious they weren't very well educated because they spoke with the slang of a backwoods farmer, but they had enjoyed a lifetime of companionship with one another and the beauty of a Michigan farming life.

The three men straightened their hats and adjusted their suspenders. The tallest of the brothers spat out his **chew** of tobacco onto the deck and began his story and song.

"This song we will sing to ya. It is the very reason we three brothers came to the state of Michigan from New York, just like all of yous. Why we decided there weren't no bear, skeeter, deep forest or even a forest fire that would keep us from this place called Michigan. After we heard this here song, this was the place we wanted ta be.

"My brothers and meself were born in Phelps, New York. A pretty enough place but not much in the way of excitement for three young, strapping lads like ourselves. When we heard this song, with the promise of Michigan's farming and all its riches, we knew it was the place we wanted ta be."

The tallest then cleared his throat and put his arms around his brothers' shoulders to lead the trio in song. The other brothers were ready and waiting to join at the sound of the first note.

"Come all ye Yankee farmers who'd like to change
your lot.
Who've spunk enough to travel beyond your
native spot
And leave behind the village where Pa and Ma
do stay."

The brother motioned for the children to join in on
the chorus. Their voices were bright, clear, and hopeful
as they thought about their new home, and they
followed the men in song.

"Come, follow me and settle in Michigan-i-a.
Come, follow me and settle in Michigan-i-a.
What country ever growed so great in such a
little time,
Just popping from nurs'ry right into like its prime,
When Uncle Sam did wean her, 'twas but the
other day,
And now she's quite a lady, this Michigan-i-a.

Upon the river Clinton just thro' the country back
You'll find in shire of Oakland the town of Pontiac,
Which springing up so sudden scar'd wolves
and bears away
That used to rove about here, in Michigan-i-a.

Come, follow me and settle in Michigan-i-a.
Come, follow me and settle in Michigan-i-a.

Or if you'd rather go to a place called Washtenaw,
You'll find upon the Huron such land ye never saw.
Where ships come to An Harbor right through
La Plaisance Bay
And touch at Typsylanty in Michigan-i-a.

99

Or if you keep going a great deal farther on
I guess you'll reach St. Josey where
everybody's gone,
There everything like Jack's bean grows monstrous
fat, they say,
And beats the rest all hollow in Michigan-i-a.

Then come, ye Yankee farmers, who've mettle hearts
like me,
And elbow grease a plenty to bow the forest tree;
Come take a quarter section and I'll be bound
you'll say.
This country takes the ragg off, this Michigan-i-a.

Come, follow me and settle in Michigan-i-a.
Come, follow me and settle in Michigan-i-a."

By the time they finished, a crowd of passengers
stood around and whooped, hollered and applauded.
    "There's truth in those words," called a bystander.
"Michigan-i-a is a place unmatched."
    Everyone cheered in agreement.
    "Michigan-i-a is the place ta be, that's fer sure,"
said an old man who was missing all his teeth but who
smiled generously with his gums.
    The children held onto the song and tried to
remember the words throughout the afternoon, making
up verses of their own and laughing at one another.
All waited and wondered what their new home truly
would be like.
    The autumn darkness came early on the deck that
evening as cold clouds gathered over the lake often
blinding out the light of the moon. The children knew
they soon would be in port and would not have to sleep

another night in steerage. But as the winds picked up, they were forced below to keep the chill from them.

Lanterns already were lit, and their abandoned berths were filled with emigrant passengers catching their sleep before continuing on their journeys in Detroit. The children sat on boxes and barrels listening to the mooing of cattle, the clucking of the chickens and the bleating of sheep while they dodged the yellow streams that oozed above them. They were just biding their time until they arrived in Michigan.

Chapter Thirteen
Kingdom Come!
Sunday, October 1, 1854

It was ten o'clock on Sunday night when the steamer finally chugged its way into the port at Detroit. The children all were happy to leave the bedbug-and-flea-infested boat. They helped carry their dwindling supplies down the gangplank and onto the dock. Mr. Smith counted to make sure they all were there while the children shivered in the cold and damp autumn air that chilled them to the bone. They watched as the clouds danced across the face of the moon casting weird reflections onto the surface of the inky, black river.

Mr. Smith handed out the bundle of blankets to help keep the children warm. He then broke off pieces of dried bread and passed the basket-bottle of water he had purchased aboard the ship trying to fill their empty stomachs.

"I am sorry there isn't more, but I need to keep the rest of the food for tomorrow morning. After that, you will be sitting down to tables filled with the abundant foods grown on Michigan farms."

The children smiled. They were tired of apples and pears, dried bread and stale cheese; and the idea of a

Michigan feast sounded good to them.

The night was dark and so was the dock. George and Sarah clung to one another while the rest huddled for warmth.

"I need to go secure passage on the train for the final leg of our journey. We will be traveling aboard the train to a place called Dowagiac in southwest Michigan. It is my hope and desire that you all will be in new country homes belonging to the fine people of that community by tomorrow evening."

"Dog-act? That's a funny name," said John as he stomped his bare feet, trying to keep them warm. "I like dogs."

"Doe-act," said another. "What's that?"

"I don't think that is what he said," commented George as he peeked from under his sister's blanket.

"The name of the town, children, is Dowagiac, pronounced 'Doe-wah-jack.'" Mr. Smith announced.

"I am told it is an Indian name, and it means a place of foraging or a place to gather food."

"That's a good name," commented Jack. "I like that ... Doe-wah-jack."

The children all repeated the name several times to themselves, as that would be the name of their new home.

"Now that we have that settled, I need to ask all of you if you can manage one more night of travel to take you to your new homes?"

The children stood silent, wrapped in their blankets and shivering in the cold, not wanting to do anything but crawl back into a nice, warm, clean bed at the Lodging House.

"Sure. I've been waitin' a lifetime for a decent bed. What's one more night?" said John, his blanket over his head, his hands buried in his pockets, and his bare toes wiggling.

"Sounds grand ta me, too," commented Jack. Slowly, all the children agreed and Mr. Smith smiled at his little crew of hopefuls.

"Now I want you all, please, to stay right where you are, because I also need to find us transportation to the train depot. Promise me you will behave yourselves, stay out of trouble, and all stay together and look after one another."

"We promise," said Sarah as she peeked out from beneath her blanket that was wrapped around her and her little brother.

"All of you?"

"Yes ..." they all chimed in sleepily.

The children watched and shivered as Mr. Smith disappeared down the dock toward the scattered lights of the city of Detroit. They decided to sit together, tucked into a circle of small boxes and large crates on the dock. The crates blocked the wind, and they shared their blankets and body heat to stay warm.

Once he was settled, Jack poked his head up over the boxes to see if he could see Mr. Smith coming back yet. Just then, a paper caught on the wind blew past his face and out over the dock into the river. Soon another old page of newsprint flew by dancing on the breeze and floating in the air above them.

As Jack sat, he watched page after page as it blew by, some sticking against their blankets and others against their faces while still others flew on the wind out into the river. The children buried their heads under their blankets, escaping the attack of the newspapers, and laughed.

John pulled some paper off a crate and stuck it under the blanket to wrap his feet and keep them warm. It was like a shower of papers that filled the air blowing in every direction.

"Some newsie went hungry tonight," said one of the older boys from under his blanket remembering how it was when he hadn't sold all his papers.

"Well, at least my feet will be warm because of it," commented John.

Jack watched as the papers blew all around them clinging to the crates and boxes. Thinking for a moment, Jack quickly jumped up and grabbed a handful from the air and then chased more down the dock.

"What ya doin', Jack?"

"Jack is an old newsie, don't ya know."

"No, I have an idea! Catch the papers!"

John jumped up to help in the fun, grabbing the sheets in midair and catching them as they hid around the corners of boxes.

Soon the boys returned with an armful of the inky sheets, which they put into a pile. John put his feet in the center of them, holding them down and warming his toes.

"Help me crumple them up," said Jack as they began balling and squashing the papers. Some of the papers Jack scrunched up and tied in the middle, and then he scooped them all together.

"Move back. Everybody move back and out of the center."

The children pulled their legs in and scooted closer to the crates and boxes, pulling their blankets snugly around them.

Jack squatted down near the pile and pulled a match from his pocket. This would leave him with only three matches to buy a meal, but begging door-to-door was better than freezing in Michigan.

Striking the match to his boot heel, Jack attempted to light the crumple of papers, but the wind was too

106

strong and the tiny flame was soon extinguished.

"Light a fire, Jack. Get another match."

"Yes, Jack, light us a fire," cried Sarah.

Jack thought for a moment. Did he dare use another match? What if ...

"Please, Jack," called George from the crack of his sister's blanket. It's freezing."

Jack hesitated for a moment and then pulled another match from his pocket. This time one of the older boys put his boot in the middle of the crumpled papers so Jack could strike the match right into the papers.
It worked!

Slowly, a blue flame grew and took hold of the papers that started to burn. The children all drew near and placed their hands over the flames to protect it and to warm themselves. It was wonderful to have warmth again as they moved closer and closer. Some of the burned paper started to float upward into the air.

Jack swatted at the flying embers. The children all laughed as more and more of the black, burnt paper rose mysteriously into the air, floating above their heads and then settling on the boxes that surrounded them.

"Hey! Hey! Hey!" hollered John. "Look!" he pointed as the edge of Sarah's blanket as it began to smoke and smolder.

Sarah quickly yanked the blanket from around her and George. As she did, the wind created by their movements ignited the edges and a white-blue flame shot into the air from it. Sarah screamed and dropped the blanket onto the wooden dock.

Boots and caps pounded on the flames, trying to put them out; but with the help of the wind, their actions only managed to spread the flames.

The girls gathered together and screamed out for help as the boys struggled. Jack grabbed hold of the edge of the blanket and flung the flaming mess over the dock and into the river. They all watched as the blanket danced in a graceful, blazing manner until it finally plunged into the water below and sent sparks up high into the air.

"Hey, you kids! What in tar-nation do you think yar doin'? Ya tryin' ta burn the dock down or something?"

A tall man in a big overcoat ran toward them, pushing them away from what was left of the newspaper fire. With one big scoop of his boot, he shoved the pile of papers off the dock and into the Detroit River. Paper embers flew in all directions and danced in the air.

"Help me catch them. What's the matter with ya?"

The children scattered in all directions at the insistence of the man. They swatted out the little sparks that were landing on the crates, boxes and the dock. The man ran and grabbed a nearby bucket that was filled with water. He splashed the water in every direction and up on the freight.

"Get them all and get them out good. These boxes you all are settled into are full of dynamite and blasting caps that are on their way to the mining camps up north. You would have blown this whole dock and all of us to Kingdom Come if I hadn't come along."

Jack stood wide-eyed in shock and swallowed hard. He

could have blown everyone to bits and the city of Detroit too.

Just then, they heard the squeaking wheels of an old wagon that was coming up the dock. Soon they could see the wagon that was being pulled lazily by a large, clomping horse. It was Mr. Smith returning with a wagon.

Surprised to see the man standing in the midst of the children, Smith jumped down from the wagon and rushed to their side.

"What's going on here?"

"All these yar children, Mister?" demanded the man who had saved them from being blown to the far side of the moon.

"Yes, they are with me. What's wrong?"

"Well, ya better keep a better eyeball on them, that's all, before they burn the city down and blow up the docks."

"I ... I ..." Smith was at a loss for words. "Didn't I tell you to behave and all stay together?"

"Yes," responded the children dropping their heads, scared and ashamed.

"Well, keep an eye on them! That's all I got ta say!" The man turned sharply and stomped away up the dock as newspapers blowing in the wind plastered themselves against the back of his long coat as he walked away.

The children snickered at the sight and Mr. Smith, though still angry, smiled too.

Chapter Fourteen
Confession

"What happened here? Who was that man? Did I not tell you to behave yourselves and not get into trouble while I was gone? I want to know the meaning of this!" insisted Mr. Smith angrily.

The wind on the dock blew cold around them, while the old gray horse that pulled the wagon stamped its foot impatiently, waiting.

"Children! Did you hear what I asked?" demanded Smith.

"I want to go home. Back to New York City," cried the voice of a little girl.

"Me, too," said another. Sniffles could be heard all around.

"Sarah, where is your blanket?"

Sarah stood silent, shivering in the wind, not wanting to get Jack into trouble.

"Speak up!" demanded Smith.

Jack stepped forward; it wasn't fair to the others. He knew he needed to be honest and confess, even if it might mean that he would be returned to New York because of his ill behavior and possible danger to the others. But he had to ...

111

"It weren't nothin', Mr. Smith," interrupted John as he stepped up and stood beside Jack. "That old sailor don't know what he's talkin' about. Just tryin' ta scare us, that's all."

"Jack, what is it? Do you have something to say?"

Jack hung his head; he could feel the tears starting to burn in his eyes. "I just wanted ta help keep everyone warm. 'Tis all."

"Don't say nothin'," insisted John, nudging Jack with his elbow.

"John, I want you to be quiet. Jack, please, continue."

Jack looked down at his boots as tears began to fall. He didn't want to go back to New York. He didn't even want to go back to the Lodging House. He wanted a home and a family and to live in the country, but he knew his Mum would be ashamed of him if he didn't stand up and be responsible for his actions and tell the truth. He knew he would be no better than a liar and would be ashamed of himself. He couldn't live with that.

Jack looked up and stared at Smith, wiping the tears from his eyes. "I just wanted ta help everyone stay warm. I just wanted ta be of help like ya asked of me."

"Yeah, that's right. He was just bein' of help. Weren't his fault the papers were blowing around in the wind. He couldn't help it. And it weren't his fault there was dynamite in those boxes, either," said John.

"Dynamite! What are you talking about?"

"And my blanket," added Sarah. "The wind caught my blanket and it blew into the river. Jack, he only tried to help. It wasn't his fault. Don't send him back to the city, Mr. Smith, please."

"Jack just tried to catch the blanket," added George, "but he couldn't 'cause of the fire. It was too hot and

112

blazin'. He was just trying to help us keep warm. Don't send him back, Mr. Smith."

"Your blanket? Dynamite? What do you mean it was blazing? Sarah, where's your blanket?"

Sarah pointed over the side of the dock into the inky, black water and burst into tears. George wrapped his arms around his sister and tried to comfort her.

"Jack was just tryin' to help."

"I'm sorry, Mr. Smith. I lit some papers with me matches, ta keep us warm. 'Tis then Sarah's blanket caught fire 'n the wind took the papers 'n scattered 'em around. 'n these boxes here, the man said, are full of dynamite and blasting caps, 'n ... I'm sorry. Don't send me back, Mr. Smith. Please, don't send me back."

Just then the driver of the wagon hit the rump of his horse with the leather reins. "Back! Back!" He clicked his cheeks and snapped his lips, and the old gray horse began to move backward.

"I ain't stayin' on no dock that's 'bout ta blow. Get loaded or I'm leavin' all of ya. Do ya hear me?" insisted the driver.

Mr. Smith stared at Jack as his red hair blew around his face in the cool wind. "I don't know what to do with you, Jack."

"Back! "**Gee**! Gee! Back!" the man directed the horse.

"Don't send me back, Mr. Smith, please."

"Ya comin', Mister, or not?" called the driver from the station wagon.

"Yes! Wait! Wait! We are coming. Children, get your things. Hurry, get loaded. We must get down to the train depot. The Night Express soon will be in."

Everyone scampered for their blankets, and Mr. Smith loaded the last hamperful of food onto the back of the wagon.

113

"I want you children to share your blankets with Sarah and George," instructed Smith.

"I'll share mine with 'em, sir," insisted Jack.

"I still have my blanket, Mr. Smith," said George proudly holding it up as he helped Sarah aboard. "Mine didn't go up like a flaming torch. I'll share mine until we get ta Dog-act."

From all around the wagon, the name "Doe-wah-jack! Dowagiac!" was shouted at George.

"You better get that name right, Georgie," called John, "or those people won't let us stay in their town."

The children all agreed as George cuddled up with Sarah in the back of the wagon, and he repeated the name Doe-wha-jack, Doe-wha-jack, over and over to himself trying to get it right.

"Jack? Where are you? We aren't finished with this yet," demanded Smith.

Jack hurried to his side afraid and not knowing what to expect. "Yes, sir?"

"Jack, you have to be more careful. Do you understand?"

"Yes, sir."

"I know you were only trying to help, but you have to think before you act and this was one of those times you didn't think."

"Yes, sir." Jack stared up at Mr. Smith, wondering when he was going to tell him he had to return to New York.

"Now hurry up! Get aboard. We have a train to catch."

"Yes, sir!" said Jack. He couldn't believe Mr. Smith was willing to overlook what he had done without there being harsh consequences. This was the first time in his whole life that he ever had told the truth and wasn't punished for it.

"Gee! Back! **Whoa!**" called the driver as he gently tapped the rump of the old gray horse, guiding it with the leather straps. "Gee! Back!" With a series of clicks and whistles from the driver, the wagon turned carefully beside the crates and boxes on the dock—backing up and turning, backing up and turning, backing up and turning.

"Gee! Back! Back! Back! Whoa!" cried the driver, until the large wagon was completely turned around.

"Gee! Gee!" he shouted, turning right off the dock onto a bumpy, rutted road that caused the cart and children to wobble from side to side. It was worse than the waves on Lake Erie. They all held on tightly to one another from fear of tumbling off.

Jack, happy and relieved that he would not have to return to the city, peeked out from beneath his blanket and watched as they passed by large, dark warehouses and small shops that lined the harbor front of Detroit.

"**Haw!** Haw!" shouted the driver, as they turned left away from the river. Small houses lined the road one after the other with their chimneys sending blue threads of smoke curling high into the cold, night sky. They traveled slowly rocking and wobbling their way onward toward the station.

Jack was just beginning to feel warm and comfortable, enjoying the ride, when the wagon started to slow and finally drew to a halt. The driver clicked and whistled at the old gray horse and spoke to it lovingly. "That's me good girl. Good job, girl. Ya got all the nice boys and girls ta the train station, now did't ya?"

Carefully standing up in the back of the wagon and trying hard not to step on anyone, Jack peeked up and over the driver and Mr. Smith. There, in the distance, he now could see the depot with its bright lanterns casting

halos into the night sky.

"This is as close as I can take ya as the horse is still a bit **skitterish** of these modern **contraptions**," said the driver.

"This will be fine," said Smith to the driver. "Children, we are here. Are you awake? Please, we must get going. The train will be in soon," pleaded Smith, trying to roust the group.

In the distance, Jack could hear loud, chugging sounds and then the clang, clang, clang of a far-off bell as the train approached on its fingers of steel.

"She's a comin'," said the driver. "That will be yer train. She be 'bout a quarter mile out. Ya can hear her bell a quarter mile out, they say."

The children slowly began moving, bumping and nudging one another until they all had poked their heads out from beneath their blankets and started to stand.

"The train!" cried Taylor excitedly as he stood and stared toward the track. "It's comin'! I can see the lamps!"

"Our train to take us to ..." George hesitated a moment. "To Doe-wha-jack," he said with a smile.

"Hey, ya got it right. Those people there might just let us stay after all," joked John.

"All right, Georgie!" they all cheered.

George grabbed hold of his sister's arm, helping her to her feet. "Hurry, Sarah. The train's a-comin'. We're going to Doe-wha-jack."

Sarah stood and pulled George's blanket up around her and hopped down. She watched as George ran ahead with Taylor to see the train.

The older children helped unload their belongings, and the basket-bottle of water was passed for everyone to drink. Jack watched as John, still barefoot, lifted first one foot and then the other, trying to keep warm.

"Good luck ta ya, children! Don't go lightin' no more fires," chuckled the station wagon driver.

Jack looked up at the man and smiled. "Good luck, son," said the driver as he slapped the rump of the old gray horse, and the wagon slowly pulled away.

Chapter Fifteen
The Michigan Central Rail Road

The children, following Mr. Smith toward the depot, watched down the tracks. They could hear the clang, clang, clang of the train's bell giving its warning, "Get out of the way. The train's coming! Get out of the way!"

They stood in awe and watched as the lamps on the front of the train grew bigger and bigger as it approached in the darkness. Bright, red sparks from the smokestack filled the air like a million fireflies.

"It looks like a fire-breathing dragon," said George.

"Yes, like a monster ready to eat us up," added Sarah as she hid her face in the blanket.

"What ya talkin' about?" snapped Taylor. "She's beautiful."

The children watched in the cool autumn night until Mr. Smith demanded that they follow him into the depot. Once he was inside, he stood by the door and counted the children as they entered.

Inside, the depot was filled with men in suits and tall hats and ladies carrying babies and pulling sleepy children along. Some of the people were waiting for the Night Express that was carrying their loved ones here to them. Other people were waiting to travel west across

119

the state of Michigan.

Mr. Smith directed the group to the ticket booth where a man in a suit sat behind a caged window with a drawer full of money in front of him. The children crowded around and stared at the man and his money. None of them ever had seen so much money in all their lives.

"Wish I could have me some of that money," whispered John to Jack.

Overhearing what was said, Mr. Smith turned around sharply and glared at the two of them.

The boys stood silent as Mr. Smith turned back and pulled out the letter of introduction that had been given to him from Mr. Nobles in Albany, and he slipped it through the bars of the cage.

Taking the letter, the man read it slowly and then looked up at Smith and the children. Without saying a word, he picked up the money drawer, slipped it under the counter, and disappeared through a door in the back of the booth.

"Excuse me. My letter? Hello? Excuse me, sir," called Mr. Smith. Smith turned to the children and shrugged his shoulders, not sure what was to happen next. They all stood silently and waited.

Soon the man returned to his caged booth without the letter. He smiled at Smith, pulled his money drawer back out, and placed it on the counter again.

"Sir, my letter of introduction. I am from the Children's Aid Society of New York City. That letter ..."

"Ya see that fella comin' out of the door over there?" said the man, pointing a bony finger at a group of men. "The one in the blue suit with all those shiny buttons on it. He's got that big, curly mustache. That man there will be taken care of ya. And good luck ta all you fine boys and girls. Good luck ta ya all."

121

"Thank you, sir. Thank you very much. Children, what do we say?"

All the children chimed in to thank the man for his well wishes. Just then a heavy hand reached out and tapped Smith on the shoulder. It was the man with all the shiny buttons. He held the letter in his hand.

"Rev. Smith, I assume. Please to make your acquaintance. You indeed are a brave man, a very brave man, to bring all these children all this way by yourself. And I am here to welcome you and these fine children aboard the Michigan Central Rail Road."

The man with the many shiny buttons wiggled his nose while he talked and twitched his mustache which was big and bushy and curled up at the ends nearly poking him in the eyes.

"Why, we thank you, sir," said Smith.

"Mr. Noble, whom you met in New York, told me to keep a sharp eye out for all of you and take care of you when you got here."

"Yes, that was very kind of him. Thank you."

"I am an agent for Michigan Central Rail Road and ... "

Just then, great billows of steam filled the air outside, and the noise of steel against steel could be heard as the train pulled to a squeaking halt. Its great wheels locked to a stop in front of the depot. The engine huffed and puffed, still breathing, pulsating with energy. The great brass bell clanged again to announce the train's arrival.

All around, people from inside the station poured out onto the platform as they watched and waited to welcome the travelers exiting the train.

Joining in the excitement, the children rushed to the platform with the crowd. There on the tracks, in a cloud of white steam, sat a great black engine with brass fittings and wheels painted bright red. Mr. Smith and the man with the shiny buttons and curly mustache joined

122

the children in awe.

"There she is. She's right on track. She sure is a fine engine, wouldn't ya say? Ya might even say she'll make the grade." The man chuckled to himself as he made railroad puns.

Mr. Smith smiled, too.

"Well, children, what do you think of your train?" asked the man.

"She's beautiful," cried Taylor. "I want to be a train engineer someday."

"Well, is that so? Well, ya got to get a good education to be an engineer. Lots to know. Lots of power behind that boiler of hers."

Taylor's eyes were big and round and full of excitement. "I know! And I still want to be an engineer!"

"Well, good for you, boy! You must be a smart young man," said the man as he rolled the end of his mustache in his fingers. "Good for you!"

"Now, children, I hope you have had a pleasant travel thus far to our fine state of Michigan."

The children stood silently, remembering the bedbugs and seasickness, the first train in New York with all its dirty smells, and nearly blowing themselves to Kingdom Come on the docks.

"But I guarantee you that your ride aboard the Michigan Central Rail Road will be the best ride you ever have had. Perhaps the best ride of your life.

"You are going aboard the 4-4-0. The classic American eight-wheeler they call her. It has two outside cylinders; you can see here." The man pointed out along the wheels. "It gives it a long wheelbase to make the ride smooth. Up top there," he pointed, "you have a wagon-top boiler. That's what's making all the steam and gives the train its power.

123

And way up front, ya even got a cowcatcher to keep you safe."

"What's a cowcatcher, Mister?" John asked loudly.

"Why, young man, a cowcatcher does just exactly what its name tells you. It catches any cows that might have the ill luck to stray out onto the tracks.

"Why, something the size of a big, old cow could throw this engine right off the track and kill every last one of you. A cowcatcher, however, out there in front and pointed like it is, can scoop a cow right off the track and roll it aside before it can cause any damage to anyone or anything."

"What happens to the cow?"questioned Sarah.

Mr. Smith chuckled to himself as he looked out over the faces of the children, every one of them curious and wondering.

"Well, little lady, the cow isn't quite so fortunate as the steam engine."

Sarah looked over to George and scowled. "That's terrible." The children all nodded their heads in agreement.

"Poor cow," added George.

"Well, children, it has been arranged for you by the owners of this fine company that you will have a passenger car to yourselves with first-class accommodations,"

"Mister, what's first class?" questioned John.

"Why, first-class accommodations are the finest passage we have. With comfortable bench seats covered with handsome green velvet cushions, and they even have backs on them. Windows that move up and down and a closed-seated privy to relieve yourself out of the sight of others.

"Now, what do you think of that?" asked the man.

The children all looked at one another. Then John

jabbed Jack in the ribs and started to laugh. "A closed privy. Now that is first class."

The children all laughed.

"Now, we will have to give the train some time after it unloads to take on some wood in its **tender** for fuel and to get its belly full of water for the boiler. But after that, you will be on your way west." The man twitched his mustache, wrinkled his nose, and gave them all a great, wide smile.

"Yes, yes. This is wonderful," said Mr. Smith. "What do you say, children?"

A round of applause was given to the man accompanied by thank yous coming from every direction.

"Now, you make yourselves comfortable in the depot and soon enough you all will be on your way." Mr. Smith shook the man's hand while the children ran inside and found places to sit on the hard wooden benches.

Nearly everyone in the train station had left with the passengers who had gotten off the train. The depot now was almost empty and each weary traveler, except George and Sarah, found a bench and spread out their blanket to get comfortable.

Jack watched as Taylor crawled up onto a bench under a row of windows. He stood looking out at the train where men in blue uniforms and holding pocket watches stood in the doorway and talked.

The time passed quickly as the wood was loaded and the train took on water. Soon the man with the shiny buttons and big mustache returned. In his teeth, he held a silver whistle that he blew sharply to get everyone's attention.

"Children! Children! Come! It's time to go!"

Everyone pulled their things together and then wiped

the sleep from their eyes. They followed Mr. Smith and the man outside to the waiting train. The steam already was beginning to fill the air with great, white puffs and the engine began to make strange, huffing noises. The man led the way, passing car after car, until they were behind the tender at the first passenger car.

"Here you have it children—first class. All aboard!" The man, crinkling up his nose and mustache, blew his whistle again.

Being careful not to trip over their blankets, the children climbed up the three steps and walked through a doorway. Jack helped Sarah and George into the car and, to their surprise, it was just as the man had said. It was beautiful. The wooden benches did indeed have backs on them. There were green velvet cushions, brass fittings and even the floor was bright and clean.

The man with the shiny buttons climbed up into the car with them. "You children have this car all to yourselves, so stretch out and get yourselves comfortable."

They cheered in delight. They never had seen anything like it. The Michigan Central Rail Road was surely nice.

Taylor pushed himself back to the railroad agent and clasped the agent's hand in both of his, shaking it. "Thank you, Mister. Now I know I definitely want ta be a train engineer. Thank you."

"Make sure you study hard, son, and perhaps someday I will ride on one of your trains."

Taylor stood frozen to the spot, imagining the possibility.

"I'll let ya ride for free, too," he said.

The man burst out in laughter, his curly mustache nearly touching the tops of his cheeks. "You're a right thinker, boy! You sure are a smart one."

Taylor smiled at the man with his shiny buttons and big bushy moustache, and then he ran down the aisle to get a seat as close to the front of the car as he could.

Chapter Sixteen
Faraway Home

Soon the children found benches of their own.
They stretched out lying full length upon the soft,
green, velvet cushions and made cozy beds with their
blankets. Some of the children used the enclosed privy
after first carefully inspecting it. Soon a long line
formed outside the privy door. Everyone wanted to see
it and how it worked even if they didn't need to use it.
It was a luxury aboard a train that was unheard of by
most travelers.

Smith counted the forty-five children just to make
sure his precious cargo was all aboard and accounted
for. He hoped that, after tomorrow, these children would
have new homes and families to look after them and
keep them safe.

"Mr. Smith," whispered a low voice. It was Sarah,
cuddled up with George who already was sound asleep.
"Mr. Smith, thank you for not sending Jack back to the
city," she said with a sleepy smile.

Smith looked down at the little, curly-haired girl and
tucked the blanket up around her and George.

"Now, don't you worry. We all will make it to
Dowagiac. I know he was only trying to help. I want you
to get some sleep now. We will be there before you

know it." Smith smiled, as he knew it wouldn't take much to find homes for the two of them, but he only hoped it would be in a home together.

Soon the train bell clanged again as it cleared the tracks and made way for the **iron horse** so it could move west through Michigan.

The sluggish chugging of the boiler soon gave way to a head of steam, and the wheels beneath them rolled round and round. No sooner had they gotten underway than a purser came through and lowered the wicks on the lamps, bringing the first-class train car into semi-darkness. After little rest the past three nights, the children sought sleep like a treasure, and found it in gentle sighs and snores.

As it passed over rivers and through dark pine forests, the train wound its way through the pleasant countryside of Michigan. The hours passed quickly, too quickly for the children, for no sooner had Jack fallen asleep than the loud clanging of the bell on the engine brought him back to his senses.

The bell clanged over and over until all the children were awake. Jack looked around as the purser entered and adjusted the wicks again bringing the train car back into full light.

"Rev. Smith," he said gently as he waited for Smith to awake and wipe the sleep from his eyes. "Rev. Smith, we are not far from Dowagiac. You might want to make sure the children have all their things together."

"What? Has it been six hours already?"

"Yes, sir, nearly that."

"Thank you. Thank you," said Smith who still was exhausted and barely able to open his eyes.

"Children. Children, please listen," he called.

Sleepy heads pulled from beneath blankets as yawns and groans of protest were heard from all the children.

"Children, we are nearly at our destination. I would like you all to please pick up your blankets. Use the privy if necessary, and prepare to leave the train as we soon are to be in Dowagiac.

"It's still nighttime," groaned John. "I want to go back to sleep."

"No, no. Now come, children. It is already morning."

"Early morning," said Jack, agreeing with his friend.

"Yes, it is very early. It is nearly three o'clock in the morning. But the train is almost to Dowagiac. Come, children. This is what you have been waiting for."

Some of them stood and stretched. Some went to use the privy one last time. Still others sat with their blanket over their heads, shielding their eyes from the lamps.

Within minutes, the train car was full of whining, tired boys and girls. Mr. Smith did his best to cheer their spirits even though he was as tired as they were.

"Look. The sun will be up soon. You will have a hot breakfast this morning.

"Girls, make sure your hair is neat and tidy. Boys, make sure your jackets are buttoned and your shirts are tucked in. We all want to make a good first impression when we arrive."

"Good impression?" questioned John. "Everyone will still be in bed sleepin' if they've got any sense."

The children laughed and gathered at the windows looking out into the night. The steam from the train's engine cast a weird fog onto the tall pine trees that surrounded them. As the wheels began to lock to a stop and caused the train to slow, the mist rose into a hundred weird shapes. The shapes floated in the air around the train car in the gloom of the night giving a frightful feeling of silence and loneliness to all the young travelers.

"Children, we have arrived."

"Where, Mr. Smith?" asked George. "It looks like we are just in a cloud."

"No, we are in Dowagiac."

Soon the back door of the train car was pulled open, and there stood a man with a slouched blue cap on his head and a full set of whiskers on his chin.

"You all be the children from New York?" the station master asked.

"Yes, that we are," said Smith as he stood and walked to greet the man.

"Well, son ... " said the man. "They sure grow their boys big in New York City, if yous be one of the children."

Mr. Smith laughed at the good-natured old man. "I am Rev. E. P. Smith from the Children's Aid Society. I supervised this trip for the children."

"Oh, I see. Ya had me worried fer a minute. Folks around here were expecting little ones, but I know a few widows that might be interested in the likes of you."

Smith didn't know what to say. He only smiled and blushed, while the older boys and girls giggled at the remark.

"Well, ya might as well be getting yourselves together. Folks around here won't be gettin' up for a few more hours, so ya'll have to camp out on the platform as this train will be headin' down Chi-ca-ge way in not so long. Unless, ya wantin' ta go find homes there. But I know there'd be some pretty disappointed people here in Dowagiac to have missed ya all."

Within minutes, the children had grabbed their blankets, straightened their hair, buttoned their jackets, tucked in their shirts and were helping Mr. Smith get everything organized.

They followed the whiskery old man, who limped when he walked, off the train. Standing in the crisp morning air, they pulled their blankets around their heads and stood in front of a small, dark, wooden depot.

"Sir, would it be possible for the children to go inside to sleep? Out of the cold?"

"Well, it would be possible if the train station were open, but ya see, it don't open up again until six-thirty. That is in three more hours."

"But surely just this one time. There are forty-five children here."

"Well, it would be all right with me, but I ain't got the key. The agent who locked up a few hours ago took the key with 'im. What would be the sense of lockin' something up if ya don't take the key with you?"

"But don't you have a key?"

"Why should I? I don't do the lockin' up. The other feller does."

"I see. I ... "

"Come on, boys and girls," said the man. "You can make yerselves at home out here on this nice platform. The outhouse is 'round back. And if ya need it, thar's a lantern hangin' here by the door. Don't need a lantern myself, ya see. I got the eyes of a cat. I walk around all the time in the dark and can see right well."

"But do you have matches for us? The lantern isn't lit."

"Well, I told ya. I didn't need it. Why would I have matches if I don't have no need for a lantern?"

Just then the train blew a head of steam and again mist filled the air.

"You all just wait. In a few minutes this here iron horse will be gone and ya can pretend to be campin' out. 'Sides, ain't none of ya haven't slept out before,

133

so I heard tell. It'll be just like New York City to ya in no time."

"But really, I must insist ... These children have come a long way."

The train's bell began to clang, clang, back and forth, ringing its warning over and over, interrupting Mr. Smith and making the children put their hands over their ears. Slowly, the wheels began to move as the Michigan Central Rail Road train once again was on its way.

As the train pulled out, taking the light with it, Mr. Smith looked around in the steam and mist for the whiskery old man. He was no place to be found and they were surrounded in darkness.

"Mr. Smith?" Sarah called out. "Are we home?"

"Well, children, we are someplace."

Smith felt around until he located the lantern by the door. "Jack, do you have any more of those matches?"

Jack pushed his hand into his pocket and felt around; just two more left. "This Dowagiac place better work out or he would be poorer than he ever had been before," he thought.

Pulling a match from his pocket, Jack struck it against the heel of his boot. The flame glowed in the darkness and Mr. Smith lit the lantern. Finally, the small, orange flame grew white, dimly lighting the platform. Huddling together around the light, the children spread out their blankets.

"Children, I can guarantee you this was not what I was expecting. But, of course, it is early. Please try to settle in and we will find our surroundings when the sun is up."

Sarah and George put their blanket beside Jack's and sat down.

"Jack?" asked George. "Do you think maybe we can

live together?"

"That would be nice," said Sarah. "If we could."

"I do't know. I never done this before. I do't know if any of us 'ill live tagether."

"Sarah and I will live together. We have to. We're real brother and sister."

"Yeah, I guess. Maybe that is what'll happen."

"But we have to, Jack, and I want you to come live with us, too. You're like a brother."

"Don't you want to live with us, Jack?"

"Yeah, it would be grand if I could."

"Jack, I want you to live with us ..." insisted George loudly. Jack could hear him begin to sniffle.

"Georgie, what's wrong?" questioned Sarah.

"I don't like it here. I'm afraid. I'm afraid out here in the night, in the dark. In the city, I know where I'm at. Here, I don't know where I am. And maybe Jack can't come live with us." George, who was tired, whined and began to cry.

"Shush! We're tryin' ta sleep," someone on the platform called out. George started to sob silently. Jack could feel his little body shake beside him.

"I don't know where I am. I don't like it here," whispered George. "It's too dark. There always is lights in the city and it's dark here."

"George, look, you can see the lantern," said Jack softly. "It's not so dark."

"But what if I have to go to the outhouse? Where is it? I can't see out there. It's too dark. Maybe a bear will eat me."

"Shush!" snapped someone. "Be quiet."

Jack stretched his leg out, reached down into his pocket and pulled out his last match. Holding it in his hand, he realized this was the last match. The last match that kept him connected to his old life, to his past, and the city.

Jack listened to poor little Georgie, tired, exhausted and afraid, who sobbed as he leaned against him.

"It's alright, Georgie," said Sarah. "It'll only be dark for a little time longer. You don't have to be afraid."

Jack reached down and touched George's hand. "Here, this is fer ya. It's me last match. So ya always will have a match, just 'n case."

In the dim lantern light, little George looked up at Jack. His eyes were red and swollen from crying, and his bottom lip quivered. George sniffed and wiped his face and nose on his jacket sleeve.

"But it's your last match, Jack," he whispered. "Just in case."

"Yea, well the 'just in case' is for you now. 'n don't worry if we don't live tagether. I don't think this place is none too big, so I know we'll be seein' each other all the time."

"That's right, Georgie. We all are going to see each other all the time," assured Sarah.

Little George nodded his head yes and took Jack's match, holding it tightly in his hand.

"Thank you, Jack. I wish you were my real brother." George reached out and hugged Jack. Sarah reached out and hugged them both.

"Hey, get off me. What ya doin'?" Jack pushed them both away and all three giggled.

"Shush!"

"Be quiet!"

"I hope a bear does eat ya." The voices called from around the platform.

"All right, children. Go to sleep," insisted Mr. Smith.

The lantern stayed lit through the rest of the night

as the children tried to sleep on the hard, wooden platform. It made them long for the soft velvet cushions of the train and the squeaky bunks of the Lodging House.

Chapter Seventeen
Dowagiac
Monday, October 2, 1854

The lantern had burned low by the time the station master arrived at the depot at six-thirty. Expecting the orphans, he carefully made his way over the mounds of blankets and lumps of children who slept peacefully in the cool morning air. He finally reached the door and found Mr. Smith, who was propped up against it, snoring loudly.

He nudged Mr. Smith with the toe of his boot, and Smith snorted and opened his eyes. It was just beginning to get light out and the cool blueness was still around them.

"You Smith?" asked the man quietly.

"Yes. Yes, I'm Rev. Edwin P. Smith," he said and yawned, stretching his arms and shaking sleep from his body. "Yes, that's me." Mr. Smith stood slowly, his body stiff from the damp night air and the hard, wooden platform.

"Why don't ya come on into the depot? I'll get the stove going and put some coffee on."

Smith nodded his head in agreement and stretched again. Moving aside, he let the man get to the door where he placed a key into the lock and turned it, clicking it open.

All around, Smith could see mounds of blankets starting to move as the children began to awaken.

"The outhouse is around back if you have need for it. If I was you, I'd get out there before all these little ones get up," chuckled the man.

"Yes, thank you. That's a good idea," said Smith as he carefully made his way over and around the heaps of children and headed back behind the depot. When Smith returned, he could smell wood smoke in the air from the stove; it was then he noticed several places on the platform were now vacant.

The man inside poked his head out the door. "Coffee will be ready in a minute. Come on in."

"I seem to be missing some children."

"Don't go worrying about them. There's nothing they can get into around here, 'cause there ain't too much around here to get into except, maybe, the swamp. Now that place has been known to harbor a few robbers and horse thieves over the years. But that ain't no place children would want to play in anyhow. Come on in."

Smith looked around. He soon would have to get what was left from the food basket and distribute it to the children, but that could wait until they all were awake. Right now, he had the time to enjoy the company of the station master.

In the woods around the depot, Smith soon heard happy voices of children playing and arguing with each other.

"Ya comin' in for coffee?"

"Yes, that sounds nice. Thank you," said Smith. Even though drinking coffee was never a habit he had gotten used to, maybe this morning something hot would help

140

him wake up.

The sun started to rise fully, Smith watched through the door as the children got up, shook the dew off their blankets and spread them flat to dry. Some disappeared behind the depot, while others went off into the woods. He watched as they walked and played curious about everything. Some even had discovered pinecones that they threw at one another. They were having a good time.

"The American House is just up the way a bit. They are expecting the children for breakfast. It is a fine establishment with a nice spread and good eatin'."

"Where will I find the church?" asked Smith. "The Presbyterian church? They were the ones who made the arrangements for the children to come."

"Well, we ain't got any Presbyterian church here in Dowagiac. Never have. Just the First Baptist Church, but perhaps the Presbyterians who meet at the Baptist church were the ones who made the arrangements. We got just a tad over 300 people who live around here; it's hard to keep track of them all.

"I do know someone put up posters about the children. Here, I think I got one." The man ran his finger over a stack of papers on his desk.

"Yep, here it is." He handed the poster to Mr. Smith who read it out loud:

Wanted! Homes for Children
A company of homeless children from New York City
will arrive here on Monday, October 2, 1854.
These children are of various ages and of both sexes,
having been thrown friendless upon the world.
They come under the auspices of the
Children's Aid Society of New York City.
The citizens of this community are asked to assist the

agent in finding good homes for them. Persons taking these children must be recommended by the local committee. They must treat the children in every way as a member of the family, sending them to school, church, Sabbath school and properly clothe them until they are 17 years old. Come see the children and hear their stories. Distribution will take place Tuesday, October 3, at the church.

"Very fine. I am glad to see these people are so looking forward to helping our children find good homes."

"Oh, yes. We ain't heard much of anything else since all this hoopla started. Lots of young farmers around here growing lots of wheat. They could use the help on the farms 'cause their own youngins aren't old enough yet to help."

"Well, yes. I understand that, but I do hope these people will offer more to these children than just treating them like farm hands and hired help."

"Oh, don't get me wrong, mister. There's plenty of love and caring to go around in this community. Those children will be treated right by us. There ain't no question of that."

"Well, that is our hope at the Children's Aid Society. To find decent and proper homes for them."

"Well, don't you go worrying about that here. After you and the children have had your breakfast, we will see to it that you get to the church and talk to the right people.

"Now, here's your coffee. Hope it's not too strong."

"Thank you," said Smith as he took the tin coffee cup in his hands. It was hot, nearly too hot to hold. Slowly he brought the black brew to his lips, blew across it to cool and carefully sipped and swallowed. The coffee was hot and thick and filled with coffee grounds. It was the worst he ever had tasted; it was so thick he could almost chew it. Smith tried hard to mask his displeasure.

"Is it all right for ya?" asked the man sincerely trying to please him.

"Yes. Yes, I don't think I ever have tasted anything quite like it before," said Smith honestly.

"Glad ta hear it. Drink up; there's plenty more where that came from."

Mr. Smith smiled and wished he simply had told the man he wasn't a coffee drinker. Looking out over the platform, he noticed the children now had tidied up, had neatly folded their blankets, and were standing about waiting to find out what was to happen next.

"I must go. I will empty the food hamper. That will tide the children over until they can eat."

"You don't want to go feedin' those children no old stale bread before they go to the American House. The people here are real glad you've come and they wanted to make it right by you. They know how hard this has been and now those children are homeless and it's our responsibility to take care of them.

" 'Sides, the women of Dowagiac would have my hide if I let you feed them stale bread with all the good cooks we have here in this neck of the woods."

Smith smiled and was grateful. These people sounded as if they were all he ever had hoped for. "Well, thank you for the coffee," he said and tried to hand the hot cup back to the man.

"No, I wouldn't think of it. Drink it up or you can take it with ya."

"Oh, you are too generous," said Smith who had hoped to get rid of the mess.

143

Joining the children on the platform with the cup still in his hand, Smith started to count heads to make sure everyone was there.

"Hey, Mr. Smith, is that coffee I'm smelling?" asked John, interrupting the count, as he came over and looked into the cup of sludge.

"I sure like coffee. Ya mind if I have some?"

"Well, John, I don't think ... "

"Please, it smells just like I like it ... "

Mr. Smith held out the cup and John took a big swallow. He waited to hear him howl but was disappointed.

"Wow! That is the best coffee ... I think I am going to like it here in Dowagiac."

"Would you like the rest, John?"

"Really? Sure." John took the cup and gulped it down. "It even has grounds in it. They say it's good fer your teeth." John smiled and showed his teeth that were all spotted and peppered with coffee grounds. "See, ya can drink it and chew it, too. Coffee sure is good."

Smith smiled and was amazed at the boy's fortitude. From behind him, the station master emerged from the depot. Noticing his empty cup, he took it from him.

"I'll get ya some more."

"Oh, no thank you, really ... We should be on our way. The children are hungry. I was just trying to take a head count to make sure we all are here."

"Well, ya can come back anytime for a cup," he said and jabbed Smith in the side.

The children began to gather together and Smith again began to count them.

"Mr. Smith, when are we going to eat?" whined one.

"Mr. Smith, I'm hungry," said another.

144

"Mr. Smith! Look!" cried one of the girls, getting his attention and interrupting the count once again. She pointed to the food hamper. It was open and turned upside down in the sand and dirt."

"What have we here? Did you see what did this?"

"It was a skinny, old, red dog. I saw him run away with the last loaf of bread in his mouth."

"Well, it's good ya weren't needin' that," said the station master. "We got a lot of old strays around here, dogs and cats both. Can't leave nothin' out. Why, I'm surprised the possums or raccoons didn't get into that before the dog."

"What's a possum and rat-coon?" asked Sarah, not liking the sound of either.

"Well, those critters are good eatin' if they don't eat your vittles first."

Sarah looked at Mr. Smith and squinted up her face. "We ain't eatin' critters for breakfast, are we?"

"Children," called Smith, "Let's go. The American House is waiting to serve us breakfast. Remember, I want you all to be on your best behavior and use your manners. Fine people of this community will be watching you, and they want to have children in their homes and on their farms who are well-behaved and well-mannered. Do you understand?"

They all nodded their heads yes. None of them wanted to do anything wrong that would keep them from finding good homes, but they sure hoped critters weren't on the menu.

"Please, pile your blankets up together and we will go have our breakfast."

Everyone followed directions. The food hamper was picked up and closed neatly and set beside the blankets.

"We will follow the station master down to the American House now. Remember your manners."

"You all don't have to be following me. Ain't much here. Just turn right out of the station and follow the tracks up to the crossroads. That's the American House. You children can just run ahead. Have fun and look around. This here is your new town now."

The children cheered and scattered running one by one and two by two. Some chased after one another while others skipped and hopped.

The station master turned to Mr. Smith. "I hope you don't mind I told them that?"

Smith frowned. "No. No, that was fine. I just wanted to count them all while they were walking, but I am sure we are all together.

"Children, wait for me outside the American House when you find where we are going," Smith called after them.

Everyone was excited. Even Jack couldn't believe that he was finally in Dowagiac; he was finally going to have a home of his own.

"Mr. Smith?" said Sarah pulling on his coat sleeve. "Mr. Smith? Mr. Smith!" she insisted, loudly.

"What? Please use your manners, Sarah."

"Mr. Smith," she began again. "Excuse me, Mr. Smith."

"Yes? What is it, Sarah?"

"Mr. Smith, I can't find George."

"What?" Smith stopped and stared at Sarah. "What do you mean you can't find George?" Looking around, Smith watched the children as they ran ahead and crossed the dirt road dodging behind trees and playing on stumps in the roadway.

"I am sure he is here, Sarah. He has just run ahead, that's all. Why don't you go find him?" Sarah looked around at the other children and back up to Mr. Smith, confused. "But I don't see him."

146

"Jack?" he called. "Will you please help Sarah find George? I am sure he is just playing up ahead."

Jack came over and took Sarah's hand. "Sure, come on," he said and the two of them ran ahead catching up with the other children, as Mr. Smith followed, talking with the station master.

"Mr. Smith! Mr. Smith! Look!" called a girl pointing at a skinny, red dog that ran across the tracks and began barking at the children in the road.

"Mr. Smith, that's the dog that stole our bread. Should we get 'im?"

Smith smiled and waved at the girl. "It's all right. We have breakfast waiting for us."

The dog continued to bark and circled the children until finally he disappeared across the tracks and into the surrounding woods.

"Those children certainly are a handful. And I see ya even got one without shoes. I'll see what I can do about that."

"Yes, but they all are good children, every last one of them, and I am sure John would appreciate some covering for his feet. That would be very nice of you."

As they walked, Smith noticed the town was built around the train station. It seemed as if the Michigan Central Rail Road gave the little settlement its reason to exist. There were a few wooden buildings that lined each side of the street, and there even was a brick building that was a mercantile business.

It wasn't a big town, and it certainly wasn't unlike most new settlements. Smith hoped the children wouldn't be bored by such a small place after having lived on the streets of New York for so long. But then, it really didn't matter what buildings were in a town. Only what the people who lived there held in their hearts mattered.

Soon, they all arrived at the American House. It was a large, wooden, two-story building that looked as if it once had been a stagecoach stop with a downstairs for eating and an upstairs with rooms to let.

"You will be staying here with the children until they are placed," said the station master. "I think you'll like it. I know the food's good."

The children stood around waiting and sniffed at the cool autumn air. They could smell the freshly baked bread and bacon frying. It smelled good.

"Can we go in now?" pleaded John. "My feet are cold."

"Forget your feet. I'm hungry," said another.

"Let me see if they are ready for ya," said the station master as he entered first and then poked his head out and motioned for them to follow.

The children piled through the door, trying their best to control their excitement and hunger.

"Manners, children, manners," reminded Smith.

Chapter Eighteen
Lost!

"Mr. Smith? Mr. Smith?"

"Not now, Jack. I need to get everyone organized."

"But, Mr. Smith. It's George. He's not ta be found. We looked all over but we can't find him no place."

"I can't find my brother," cried Sarah loudly. "I can't find Georgie."

"What do you mean he can't be found? He has to be here." Smith looked out over the crowd of children who were finding places to sit while women wearing aprons brought great bowls of fried potatoes and platters of eggs and bacon to the tables.

"I can't find my brother, Mr. Smith."

"Now don't you go worrying none, missy. He hasn't run off, too far," said the station master. "We will find him; just dry up those tears."

"Jack, perhaps we left him down at the depot or maybe in the outhouse. Would you mind going back to look?"

Jack frowned and stared down at the steaming bowls and platters of food that were waiting for him. He was hungry, as usual.

"Yea, sure," he grumbled. "Just save me somethin' ta

eat, that's all."

The station master reached over and grabbed a couple slices of bread off a plate for Jack. "Here, son, just in case."

Jack smiled. "Ah, that's grand of ya, Mister," he said and quickly snatched up the bread. Then he turned and exited.

The station master picked up Sarah and put her on a chair beside him. "Here, you stay right here next to me and they'll find that brother of yours in no time.

"That Jack sure is a help. Why, if I didn't have a house full of children of my own at home, I wouldn't mind much if he'd come and live with me. I could always use an extra pair of hands down at the depot."

"Yes, Jack is a very good boy," said Smith, distracted by concern for his lost traveler. Smith stood and began counting the children again. He wanted to make sure George was the only one missing.

Some of the town's people now began to push through the doorway of the American House. Trying to get a better look, they stood and watched as the children ate.

"Mr. Smith?" called a voice. "Ya think I can get some coffee?" It was John.

"Coffee!" snapped an older woman who was serving. "For a youngster like you? It will stunt your growth. Now drink up your milk and be quick about it."

John stared at the woman who had a stern look on her face; he hoped he wouldn't be going to live with her.

"Children, when you finish your breakfast, please remember your manners and thank the ladies for all their hard work and kind efforts. Also, I do not want any of you to leave the room; it seems that some of the town's people already are here for a visit."

The children looked around realizing for the first time that they were being watched. Some of the town's people now were seated on the steps that led upstairs, silently watching the children. Some even stood out-of-doors and peeked in through the windows at them. It made the children feel very uncomfortable.

Jack soon returned, his face red from running. "Mr. Smith. I couldn't find George no place. I looked 'round the station 'n I checked the outhouse. He ain't no place ta be found."

"Thank you, Jack. Here, come take my place and eat. Thank you for looking." Mr. Smith stood and Jack slid into his seat.

Sarah overheard what Jack had said and began to cry again. "I want Georgie. I want my brother."

"Children, excuse the interruption. Excuse me, please." Smith moved to the front of the room so everyone could see him while the children gobbled down their breakfast.

"It appears that one from our company has gotten himself separated from us. Have any of you seen George this morning? Any of you? Any time this morning?"

"George?" the children whispered his name.

"Georgie?" questioned John loudly. "Ya, I saw him this morning."

"Maybe he got eaten by a bear!" said another.

"Children, please! I need your help."

"He and Sarah slept beside me last night," said Jack, "and they both were there when I got up this morning."

"Fine. He made it through the night in our company."

"He said he had to use the outhouse when he got up," said Sarah wiping tears from her eyes. "He said he was mighty cold, too, so I let him take the blanket."

"Well, I saw him out back behind the outhouse all wrapped up in his blanket. That was right before we left. He was playing with a skinny, old dog," added John.

"He was fine then. He even threw those 'cone' things at me and then ran and hid in the trees. He was laughing and everything."

"Anyone else?"

The room was silent.

"I will get a group of the men together," said the station master as he got up from his seat. "I hope that boy didn't go playin' up around the swamp. Been more then one body turned up drowned down there over the years."

Upon hearing this, Sarah began to cry, "I want my Georgie!"

One of the women who stood near rushed over to Sarah and pulled her into her arms, cuddling her.

"What's a matter with you saying something like that around this little girl? Where's your sense? Come on, missy. You can come with me. They will find your Georgie. Shame on you!" snapped the woman at the station master.

"I didn't mean to upset the child. It's just that the swamp is a dangerous place and ..."

"Stop it right now and don't say another word," she said and shook her finger in his face.

"You poor child. Come all this way and now your little brother has come up missing. You just stay with me. I'll keep you safe and they will find George in no time."

"You men go on now and find that little boy," said a tall woman in a white apron. "We will keep an eye on the children; 'sides, it will give us a chance to get to know them."

"Thank you. Thank you for your kindness," said Mr. Smith as he rushed outside to join the search. The adult men from the town already had gathered, and the older boys and girls joined in too.

Jack quickly jammed food into his mouth, hardly chewing, not wanting to be left behind, but still wanting to eat.

"Young man, is that any way ta be eatin' at a proper table? Ya're eating like a gluttonous dog!"

Jack swallowed hard and swallowed again, trying to get the food down his throat.

"Here, have yerself some milk and ya be mindin' yer manners at this table." The woman poured Jack a glass of milk.

Jack took it and gulped it down until the food began to slide down his throat more easily.

"It's just I'm in a hurry. I got ta go with the rest of 'em and help find George. George, he's like a brother ta me."

"Boy? Ya be a son of Ireland?" asked the woman, her accent, too, now obvious.

"Yes, ma'me, I am. Came ta America but five years ago with me Da and Mum from County Clare."

"After the potato crop failure no doubt?" asked the sharp-faced little woman. It was the same with me. I'm here from Kerry. No one told me thar'd be a famine child along with these children.

"Now, son, I apologize fer slowin' ya down. Ya be hurrin' along and help with that lost little one. Ya have a good heart, ya do, and I don't want ta be holdin' ya up none.

"I should have known ya be Irish with that handsome red hair and freckles of yers. Ain't seen nothin' like it in a long while. Now, son, hurry along 'n don't be wastin' time."

Jack smiled at the lady who stood and stared at him with a smile on her face as she watched him eat.

Jack helped himself to more fried potatoes and drank some more milk. Finally, he grabbed a handful of bacon and crammed it into his pocket for a snack, just in case.

Looking around, he could see some of the women who had helped serve now sat at the tables with children and chatted with them. Some of the other town's people also had joined them. Hoping to find good homes for themselves, the children all were using their best manners.

Jack spied Sarah and watched as she now sat in the kitchen doorway with the lady who had rescued her eating and talking as if nothing had happened.

Quickly, Jack got up, slipped out the door and ran down the dirt road toward the depot. In the woods all around him, Jack could hear George's name being called over and over.

At the station, the whiskery old man who walked with a limp and had eyes like a cat, now stood talking to Mr. Smith and the station master.

"Yep, that's the boy. Just 'bout six or seven years old, he was. Up over the creek bridge walkin' all by his lonesome and wrapped up in a blanket. I wondered at the time if he was one of your orphans, but he had an old, skinny, red dog followin' him and I thought maybe he was one of ours. I called to him, but he didn't answer. He was just playin' with that old dog and havin' a good ol' time. Thought maybe he could be goin' swimmin'. I was a bit concerned at the time 'cause the current is runnin' fast, and the water is high and cold from all the rain we had last week."

"Thank you. Thank you very much for your information," said Mr. Smith.

"We better get down to the bridge and check it out," said the station master.

Having overheard the men's conversation, Jack poked his head into the depot. "I bet George was playin' with that old dog and got himself turned 'round, out behind the depot. I'd bet ya me last match on it."

"This here town is easy to get turned around in. It's laid out along the tracks, and it don't run straight north and south. I bet ya that is what happened," agreed the station master.

"Which way ta the bridge, Mister?" questioned Jack.

"Turn left and follow the tracks. They will bring ya right to it."

Jack dashed out the door, running as fast as he could and leaving the men behind.

When Jack got to the bridge, there, down below near the water's edge, stood a skinny, red dog looking out over the creek and barking. Startled by Jack's appearance, the dog turned and ran toward him, baring his teeth and snarling. As Jack drew nearer, the dog growled louder.

"It's alright, boy. Have ya seen me friend George?"

The dog held its ground, but its tail began to wag when he heard Jack's kind voice. "Come on, boy. Where's George?"

Jack reached into his pocket, grabbed the bacon he had taken from the breakfast table, and tossed it to the dog that quickly gobbled it up and waited for more.

"No more. Now let me pass," said Jack lifting his hands and showing the old dog there was no more food. The dog stood and stared. Dropping his ears, he began to wag his tail. Then he turned quickly and ran back down to the creek's edge and started barking again. Jack followed.

"George! George! Where are ya?" called Jack as he looked out over the cold, black, deep, flowing creek. The dog barked and paced back and forth.

"Georgie!" pleaded Jack. "Where ya be?"

Just then on the bridge above, Jack could see Mr. Smith and the station master catching up to him.

The dog continued barking in the same spot, and Jack looked out along the shore until finally he spied something in the water. It looked like a blanket. George's blanket! It was caught in the knobby fingers of tree roots from the water's edge. The blanket, trying to free itself from the roots, spread out on the current just below the surface of the water.

"George!"

Jack went cold and was filled with fear. Lying flat on the ground alongside the tree, he reached out and tried to loosen the blanket and pull it to the surface. But it was no use. Tears burned in Jack's eyes as he thought about George, possibly being drowned down there in the cold, black water.

"George!" he cried.

Not being able to free the blanket, Jack quickly yanked off his shirt, boots, and pants and lowered himself into the water along the creek's edge.

"Jack!" hollered Mr. Smith as he and the station master made their way down below the bridge. "Get out of there! What are you doing?"

Jack, ignoring Smith and fighting the current, pulled himself along the shore holding onto tree roots and weeds until he reached the blanket. He plugged his nose and lowered himself beneath the surface. There, on his knees, he searched with his hands in the muck for George.

In an instant a hand reached down into the water and grabbed Jack by the hair, yanking him to the surface.

"What do you think you're doing?" shouted Smith, angrily shaking Jack by the hair as he lay along the shore holding him.

Gasping for air, Jack reached for the tree roots and at the same time snagged the blanket loose. The blanket caught up around his arm and wrapped itself around Jack, pulling him into the current and from Smith's hold. The water swirled and churned around him, the force tying and wrapping him in the blanket like a cocoon.

"Jack!" screamed Smith. "Hang on! We will get you!"

"Hold on, boy. We're coming."

Jack could hear the dog barking as the current tugged him along and the heavy wet blanket weighed him down. Cold water splashed into his mouth and started to fill his lungs as he gasped for air and struggled to keep his head above the water, but it was no use. The blanket was just too heavy.

Quickly, an arm reached out and grabbed hold of Jack around the neck, yanking him to the surface and pulling him to shore. It was Mr. Smith who was stripped to his long johns.

The station master was leaning against a tree with a broken limb and helped to pull the two to safety.

Jack crawled up onto the mud and weeds, coughing and spitting, wrestling to pull free from the blanket that entangled him.

"George! It's George!" Jack chocked out with the words. "'Tis his blanket. He must be down there drowned."

Smith, standing on the shore in his long johns, turned instantly and dove back into the swiftly moving creek. Fighting the current, he too searched the muck on his knees to find George.

Jack watched and shivered, his teeth chattering in the cool autumn morning as Smith, with the help of the station master, dove into the water over and over until both men were exhausted.

The skinny, old, red dog, having at last stopped his vigil of barking, sat silently and watched the men. He

160

came to Jack's side and lay close to keep him warm. Jack wrapped his arms around the dog, and they both sat sadly and waited.

Soon, some of the other children, having followed the tracks from the train station, found their way to the creek bridge. They helped to search the shore and some even followed the station master back up the creek to the millpond to see if, perhaps, little Georgie's body would show up there.

By this time, everyone had started to give up hope. It was late afternoon now, and Mr. Smith still had to meet with the town's people of Dowagiac concerning the placement of the children that was to be held the next morning.

It was hopeless Smith thought to himself. If George had found his way into that cold, deep creek, none of them probably would ever see him again. Smith soon came away from the water's edge, quietly picked up his clothes, and started to walk back up to the bridge without saying a word to anyone. The laces on his boots flapped loosely as he sloshed in his wet long johns back toward the train station.

Jack picked up his clothes, too, and followed silently; the old, red dog stayed close to his side.

At the depot they dried off, trying to wipe the sadness from their faces as they dressed.

When the station master returned, he took the great coffee pot from the back of the woodstove where it had been simmering all day and poured Smith a cup. This time Smith took it and drank it all without a word of complaint.

Jack watched out the window and waited for Mr. Smith as the skinny, red dog lay peacefully on the platform in the warm autumn sun.

Chapter Nineteen
Poor Georgie!

By the time they returned to the American House, the dining room was empty. But up the road they could see horses and wagons standing in front of a large wooden building.

Jack followed Smith there where they found the children with long, sad looks on their faces as they sat together on benches. They were surrounded by the town's people who were standing, singing a song of hope.

When they entered, Mr. Smith was escorted to the front of the room where he looked out at the eager faces of the children and town's people.

Clearing his voice and fighting back his own tears, Mr. Smith began.

"I am afraid that we have lost one of our own today. We have searched the woods and have not found him. We have searched the creek and the millpond, and yet he is lost. It is with great sadness that I say this because George was a fine little man and will be sorely missed."

Sobs and sniffles were heard around the room, and women took hankies from their sleeves and wiped their eyes. Here and there the men honked their noses.

In the back of the room, little Sarah stood and cried out in hurt and anger. Tears fell from her eyes as she ran out the door followed by the woman from the American House who had taken charge of her.

"Even though this is a sad occasion, this is not what we have come to your community to share. We all have come together here in Dowagiac to find homes for these fine young boys and girls.

"I will not take up your time with small talk. I will simply tell you that commencing tomorrow morning, Tuesday, October 3, we will begin the distribution of the children into your community.

"Most of you have spent time this day with the children and some of you already have made your decisions. Tomorrow morning you may meet with me here, and I will be available to receive your applications of placement and interview all prospective parents and employers. As you know, it is my goal to match you with children the best I can. I also will speak with each child who is requested, to make sure that child would be pleased to reside with you. This way, it will be considered a happy match for both parties.

"At this time, I will read to you the indenture-adoption forms, the agreement you must sign if you are interested in taking a child.

"The form reads: 'I, hereby agree to provide for ... , and this is where we will put the child's name ... , until the said child reaches the age of 17 years, according to the following terms and conditions.

'To care for him in sickness and health, to send him to school the entire free school year until he reaches the age of 14 years, and thereafter, during the winter months at least, until he reaches the age of 16 years; also to have him attend church and Sunday school when convenient, and to retain him as a member of your

164

I, hereby agree to provide for..., and this is where we will put the child's name in..., until the said child reaches the age of 18 years, according to the following terms and conditions.

To care for him in sickness and health, to send him to school the entire school year until he reaches the age of 14 years, and thereafter, during the winter months at least, until he reaches the age of 16 years; also to have him attend Church and Sunday School when convenient, and to retain him as a member of your family until he reaches the age of 17 and thereafter for the final year, until the age of 18, to pay the boy monthly wages in addition to his maintenance, the amount thereof to be determined by the Children's Aid Society.

In case the child proves unsatisfactory, you agree to notify the Society pending his removal, to keep him a reasonable length of time until the Society can collect him. You must also agree to keep him, at all time well supplied with clothing as he was when your received him.

X _____

family until he reaches the age of 17 and thereafter for the final year, until the age of 18, to pay the boy monthly wages in addition to his maintenance, the amount thereof to be determined by the Children's Aid Society.

'In case the child proves unsatisfactory, you agree to notify the Society and, pending his removal, to keep him a reasonable length of time until the Society can collect him. You also must agree to keep him, at all times, as well supplied with clothing as he was when your received him.'

"And it is here where you will sign and date it or make your mark. Also, I would like to add that if the child is not happy where he has been placed, the child has the right to contact us in New York City for removal or request a placement elsewhere in your community. Are there any questions?"

"Is there a chance we can take one home with us tonight?" asked a man from the back of the room.

"No, the children will stay together this evening at the American House. All placements will begin tomorrow. Any more questions?" Mr. Smith looked around the room; everyone seemed to be satisfied.

"If there are no more questions, children, if you would please all come and gather together up front here with me so we may properly thank these fine people of Dowagiac for their kindness with a song."

Quietly, sadly, the children gathered at the front of the room. Sarah had returned; her eyes were red and swollen from crying. Together, the children stood united and sang.

"Come, ye weary, heavy laden,
Lost and ruined by the fall;
If you tarry till you're better,
You will never come at all."

That evening at the American House, the children were sad and quiet as they ate a light supper of soup and bread. When they finished, the tables soon were removed from the dining room to make way for the children to sleep on the floor.

Both Jack and John took turns watching over Sarah, who was quiet and withdrawn for most of the evening. She tried to be brave and accept what had happened. When she lay down and Georgie wasn't there, she sobbed uncontrollably.

Mr. Smith, exhausted from the day's experience and all the travel, took a room upstairs to himself. As soon as the children were accounted for and tucked in; he, too, went to bed.

Jack was restless, rolling and tossing as he listened to Sarah crying until she finally fell asleep. He wished there was something he could do or say, but George was gone and that was all there was.

The clock on the mantel in the dining room sounded ten chimes as he rolled over and counted them, wondering if any of the people in town might be willing to take him as a placement. Perhaps the Irish woman who liked his red hair. Perhaps not.

Jack rolled, tossed and turned on the hard wooden floor, but he couldn't get comfortable or stop his mind from thinking. Finally, he quietly got up and, with the light of the moon streaming through the windows, made his way over the piles of blankets with arms and legs sticking out in every direction. He stood at the door.

Turning the lock and lifting the latch ever so

167

carefully, he stepped out onto the stoop into the cold night air and pulled the door closed behind him.

The sky was clear with not a cloud to be seen, and the moon was bright and full. He could hardly believe there were so many stars. Jack felt as if he could just reach out and scoop them up in his hands. "There never was a night like this in the city," he thought. It never got dark enough to really see the stars, and the smoke from coal fires in every tenement and flat kept a constant haze in the air.

A cool autumn wind blew making Jack shiver. Leaves pulled from the trees that surrounded the little settlement, danced on the wind as they were blown over the crossroads and through the town.

Jack sat on the stoop and placed his chin on his knees, thinking and staring out into the night. Soon his eyes adjusted to the light of the moon. He was able to make out the different buildings of the tiny town and could see the outlines of their barns behind them. The whiskery old man from the train station was right. At night, if you look really hard, you didn't need a lantern to see. Perhaps he had eyes like a cat, too.

Jack sat and watched up the road, and suddenly he could see something approaching. Blinking his eyes in the dark, Jack watched as a tall, shadowy form with something following it made its way up the road. It didn't look like a man. It was something else— something with a big tail trailing behind. The form got bigger and bigger as it drew closer to the American House.

Jack watched. It was large on top, too large for a man, but it had two legs and seemed to walk with a limp. Jack quickly stood and turned, lifting the latch of the door and heading back into the safety of the dining room.

"Boy!" called a harsh, low voice from out of the darkness.

"Boy! I want you ... "

Jack was scared. Who was calling to him? Pulling the door open, Jack could see the figure in the moonlight. As it got closer and closer, something was following at its heels.

"Boy!" shouted the voice. "What in tar-nation is the matter with you? I said for you to wait. I see ya there in yar long johns," snapped the voice.

Jack stood frozen to the spot and turned slowly. There, standing at the bottom of the steps of the American House, was the old man with the whiskery chin from the train station. In his arms, with his arms and legs wrapped around the man, was George. Following closely behind was the old, skinny, red dog.

"This here youngin' belong with you all? This the boy ya lost?" The man pulled George's arms and legs lose from around him and swung him around. The movement woke George up. George stood down and wiped the sleep from his eyes. He was exhausted.

"George! George! Oh, it's Georgie." Jack jumped up and down in his excitement and grabbed George, giving him a big hug. "We thought you were a goner, George. We gave up hope."

"I found him up near the swamp. He had lit himself a little fire and was tryin' ta keep himself warm. I been out all day lookin' for this boy. It got ta bothering me because I had passed by him out on the bridge and didn't stop for a chat.

"He looked too smart to have gotten himself drowned in that old creek. I just knew he was around someplace. I'm sure glad he had a match for a fire or else he'd still be out there lost.

"I knew the boy would be fine ... My cat eyes led me

right to him. Now, go get that Reverend of yours and tell him I got something for him."

Jack turned and opened the door and quickly made his way over the lumps of children to the stairs, taking them two at a time. At the top, Jack could see a strip of lamplight coming from underneath a door. He quietly knocked on the door. "Mr. Smith?" he whispered loudly.

The door creaked open and Smith poked his head out. "Jack? What is it? You should be sleeping."

"Mr. Smith, it's George."

"Yes, I know it has been a very sad day. I was proud of you today; however, down there at the creek, it was very dangerous."

"No, it's not that ... "

"I know you probably are having a hard time sleeping ... "

"Mr. Smith. It's George! He is outside with the whiskery old man from the train station. He found George in the swamp. He's alive!"

"What?"

"Yea! They're downstairs waiting."

Mr. Smith closed the door quickly, and Jack could hear him scrabbling around and pulling on his clothes. Soon the door flew open. Smith pushed Jack out of the way and ran down the stairs, making enough noise to wake everyone.

Jack followed Mr. Smith outside where George and the old man sat talking to the old, red dog and scratching its head.

Smith grabbed George up in his arm and hugged him.

"It's a miracle! It's a miracle! Thank you for bringing him back to us."

Mr. Smith then grabbed the whiskery old man and hugged him, too.

"I'm hungry!" whined George.

"Me, too," agreed the old man. "Child searchin' can sure build up a mighty hunger."

Just then, Mr. Bock, the owner of the American House, pulled the door open. He held a lantern. "What is going on down here? There is enough noise tonight to wake the dead." The man looked down and shined his lantern on George. "Is this the drowned child?"

They all followed Mr. Bock back inside. They made their way around the blankets of sleeping children to the kitchen where they closed the door and celebrated.

Chapter Twenty
Placement
Tuesday, October 3, 1854

The next morning when the sun started shining through the windows of the American House, the children awoke to the wonderful smells of yet another hot breakfast that was being prepared in the kitchen.

The children were tidying their blankets and preparing themselves for the day. Some went outdoors to use the outhouse, while others helped get the tables put into place for the morning meal. Speaking softly to one another, none mentioned George's name because they didn't want to upset Sarah again. Jack watched and only smiled, not wanting to give away the secret.

Some of the women came into the dining room. They carried large bowls of warm water for the children to wash. They crowded around and splashed the sleep from their eyes. The girls helped each other to re-braid their hair, and the boys scrubbed their heads, making sure they were clean.

Soon, Mr. Smith came downstairs to greet the children and with him, to everyone's surprise, he brought little George.

Sarah pushed through the crowd of children and wrapped her arms around her brother, tears of joy filling her eyes.

The excitement spread around the room, and soon the women from the kitchen joined the children in the happy surprise.

By the time the mantel clock struck eight o'clock, everyone in the small town knew little Georgie was back where he belonged.

Sarah held onto her brother and hugged him over and

over until George finally pushed her away. She followed him everyplace, even when he went to the outhouse, to make sure he didn't get lost again.

After breakfast the children lined up and followed Mr. Smith down the street to the wooden church building; it was time for them to find new homes.

Many people had gathered and followed the children into the building. Mr. Smith waited patiently for all the adults to be seated on the benches before he marched the children up the center aisle to the front for everyone to see. The boys lined up on one side of the room, the girls on the other.

"Good morning to you. I trust you all have heard our happy news. Our lost little one was returned to us late last evening. It was a miracle, and we are grateful to have him back in our company."

The people all smiled and nodded their heads in agreement.

The whiskery old man stood in the back of the room with the old, skinny, red dog at his side. He had a great smile upon his face, proud of his part of the miracle.

"I want to thank you all for coming this morning and supporting the Children's Aid Society in helping us find homes for our young ones.

"Now, those of you who have taken an application to apply for the children, come forward at this time, please."

The town's people quickly stood and came forward, some meeting with Mr. Smith and others talking with the children. Jack stood and waited, wondering if anyone would chose him, but no one came forth. He stood beside John and George as men and women from the community spoke with the other children. Some smiled and laughed; others frowned and stared. But all passed them by.

One man who appeared to be a farmer did approach Jack grabbing at his arms to check his muscles to see if they had enough strength to work in the fields. The man then moved from boy to boy, passing over George completely, until finally settling on one of the oldest boys in the group.

Some of the women looked over the girls checking their hands for working calluses to see if they were lazy or would be willing to help around the house. In a large household, there always was room for one more pair of hands to help with the chores.

One old couple stood before John and reached up forcing his mouth open. They tried to run their fingers along his teeth. Fighting back, John snapped his jaws shut nearly catching their fingers in his mouth.

"What ya think yar doin'? Keep yar hands out of my mouth. I ain't goin' with ya!" insisted John as he turned away. The old couple, insulted, left the room without taking any child with them at all.

Jack waited as one by one the children left the line with their new families; yet no one came forward for him. John and George continued to stand unwanted beside him, too. They each were afraid there would not be a place for them in the hearts and homes of the people of Dowagiac.

The station master soon came in and smiled at Jack. Then he went over to George. Stooping down, he gave George a big hug to welcome him back.

Then he went to John and, from an old cloth bag, he pulled out a pair of worn boots to cover John's bare feet. Happily, John pulled them on and carefully laced them up. They were too big for him, and the ties were worn and nearly broken through; but they were better than going without.

Jack waited and hoped for the station master to look

his way again thinking what it might be like to live with his family and help at the train station. But Jack's hopes faded as the man turned and walked away. He watched as the station master headed toward the door pausing to shake hands with Mr. Smith. Soon, the Irish woman from the American House entered, and she joined the men in conversation.

Jack could hardly stand it any longer. All his hopes and dreams of a new home in this faraway place were nearly gone. He tried hard to fight back his feelings. He knew he couldn't cry because that would mean he had lost all hope and probably would have to return to New York and a life he no longer wanted. He had to believe there still was a place for him here.

Soon the Irish woman walked toward him followed by the station master; they both smiled politely. Jack stood tall, wanting to make a good impression in hopes the woman might be interested in taking in a boy from her own country. But then the two passed him by and turned toward the girls' line. She probably had a large family of her own and needed the help of a girl; Jack consoled himself, disappointed.

Jack stood and waited along with John and George as the line of boys and girls got smaller and smaller. He couldn't understand what was wrong, why no one wanted him.

The station master soon returned to the boys' line and chatted with George and joked with John. At his side again was the woman from Ireland.

"Jack?" said the station master. "I hear you have met my wife? She too is from Ireland.

"You know, I have watched you ever since you arrived at the station. You always were a big help to Rev. Smith and all the younger children, too. You're a good boy, and both my wife and I have taken a shining to ya.

"We wondered if you'd be interested in working in the train depot with me? And taste a bit of Irish cookin' again?"

The man's wife stepped forward and smiled, glowing with hope and love. "We have a houseful of children, as is, 'n it'll be a snug fit. But we would be happy ta have ya in our family. Ta be part of us. If ya would like that."

Surprised, Jack could hardly breathe. Someone did want him! "Me? Ya want me? That would suit me just fine," said Jack as a big grin spread across his face.

"Oh, that would be grand," said the woman as she reached out and hugged him. The station master smiled and slapped Jack on the shoulder. "Glad ta have ya aboard, son."

George, hearing Jack had found a new home was happy, surely he and Sarah would go live with him, after all Jack was like his big brother. But George was soon disappointed when he learned there was no room at the station master's house for two more children.

By Thursday morning, October 5, Rev. Edwin. P. Smith had found homes for another thirty-seven children in Dowagiac and the surrounding areas, but there still was no home for George and Sarah.

It was then the Presbyterian minister offered to take the older children for future placement. Records show that a few boys were bound to trades, but most insisted on being farmers. One boy went to live with a physician, a girl named Meg was adopted by a wealthy farmer, and John, once known as Smack, found a home in a Quaker settlement.

The smallest of the children, nine in all, now prepared to board the Michigan Central Rail Road with Rev. Smith.

George and Sarah slowly made their way to the train with hopes Jack would come to say "good-bye." George was sad to leave his friend and tears rolled down his cheeks. Sarah tried to comfort him, but it didn't help.

Suddenly, Rev. Smith stooped down and whispered, "Look who's coming." There on the road a wagon quickly approached with Jack standing in the back wildly waving his arms and shouting. "Reverend Smith, wait! Wait!"

A smile came to George's face. "I knew he'd come! I knew it!"

Soon the station master joined them as the wagon pulled up and Jack jumped down from the back.

"Reverend Smith," said the station master, "I would like you to meet my brother, Peter, and his wife, Rachel."

Reverend Smith watched as the man carefully helped his wife down from the wagon. Jack quickly stood beside his new Da, a great grin upon his face.

"Reverend Smith, my brother and his wife are from the next community over and they have no children of their own. And this new son of mine, Jack, has made such a fuss about these two little ones, George and Sarah, not having a home, I thought, if it would be all right with you perhaps the children might come home with them, and be near Jack.

George and Sarah ran to Jack and wrapped their arms around him and jumped up and down in their happiness."

Soon the papers were signed and Sarah and George climbed aboard the wagon with their new family as they waved good-bye to the others and started for their new home.

Jack waved from the depot platform as he helped his new Da see the Michigan Central, the Orphan Train of 1854, on its way. Rev. Smith sat near the window, a smile upon his face, with only seven children remaining to find homes for in Chicago and Iowa.

Epilogue

Not all the orphans who traveled west over the next 75 years were as fortunate as those who traveled on the first orphan train. Not all of them found homes; and not all homes were satisfactory, but as one of the orphans recorded years later: "Most of the town's people were very good people and were proud of the children they adopted."

The Emigration Plan, or placing-out system with the Children's Aid Society, continued until 1929. At least 150,000 children were placed-out during its years of operations. The exact number of children resettled, however, cannot be established with exact certainty as records were not perfectly kept (as in Jack's case) and many have been lost over the years. Some historians estimate the number of children placed may be closer to 250,000.

Charles Loring Brace's contribution of making the family an asset and not a liability to society changed the lives of thousands of children.

Edwin P. Smith ended his report concerning the trip to Dowagiac by stating: "On the whole, the first experiment of sending children west is a very happy one."

No surviving documents from the Children's Aid Society's early years expresses a shred of doubt about that statement.

In 1917, the last time the Children's Aid Society checked on the children it had placed during the past years, the children who previously had been considered "delinquent, useless, homeless vagabonds, disposable and surely bound for complete corruption on the streets of New York City," were successful in many fields. The report said that: "Placement of these children has given us a governor of a state, a governor of a territory, two members of Congress, two district attorneys, two sheriffs, two mayors, a Justice of the Supreme Court, four judges, two college professors, a cashier of an insurance company, twenty-four clergymen, seven high school principals, two school superintendents, an auditor general of a state, nine members of state legislatures, two artists, a senate clerk, six railroad officials, eighteen journalists, thirty-four bankers, nineteen physicians, thirty-five lawyers, twelve postmasters, three contractors, ninety-seven teachers, four civil engineers, and many business and professional men, clerks, mechanics, farmers and their wives, and others who have acquired property and filled positions of honor and trust. Nor would the roll call be complete without mention of our four army officers and 7,000 soldier and sailors in their country's service."

** During the time of the Orphan Train era, none of the agencies involved in the placement or placing-out of children actually used the term Orphan Train(s) in any of their official records.

** E. P. Smith was considered a "city preacher" and perhaps was not even professionally trained in that field. After extensive research, I was unable to find any formal documentation concerning the personal life or professional education of Rev. E. P. Smith.

About the Author

Janie Lynn Panagopoulos is an historian, lecturer and award-winning author. She has written a number of acclaimed historical fiction novels for young readers, and is a noted speaker nationally. Her humor, research, attention to detail and real-life stories help readers of all ages understand what it might be like to live in a different period of time. Writing stories specifically designed as teaching tools, she captures the spirit of history in a way that both entertains and enlightens. Students with whom she has shared her many adventures have nicknamed her "Indiana Jane." She was the recipient of the 2000 Michigan Author Award, and her books have won several Readers Choice Awards. She lives in Roscoe, Illinois, with her husband, Dennis. They have two sons, Christopher and Nicholas. www.jlpanagopoulos.com

About the Illustrator

Carolyn R. Stich's illustrations capture the wonderful characters in Panagopoulos' *A Faraway Home: An Orphan Train Story*. Known for her attention to detail and expressive characterization, Stich has received recognition for her work throughout Michigan. Other books illustrated by Carolyn Stich are Andy Gregg's *Paul Bunyan and the Winter of the Blue Snow*; Shirley Neitzel's *Liberty and Justice for All*, Jane Stroschin's *Atsa and Ga, a story from the high desert* and Ragene Henry's *The Barefoot Boys Of Fayette*. Married and the mother of two children, Carolyn resides in Holland, Michigan. www.carolynstich.com

Charles Loring Brace
1826-1890

Charles Loring Brace was born June 19, 1826, in
Litchfield, Connecticut, to a well-educated and
prominent family.

In 1842, he began his studies in Humanities and
Religion at Yale University. By 1848, at age twenty-two,
he relocated to New York City to complete his studies at
the Union Theological Seminary, where he saw the needs
of the underprivileged for the first time, and he found
his calling.

He was horrified when he realized the New York City
police and Metropolitan police arrested children, some
as young as five years of age, and locked them up in
adult prisons. Brace took a stand. "These children were
not criminals," he argued to anyone who would listen,
"but victims of miserable economic and social
conditions."

About this time, official records in New York City
showed that 4,000 inmates under the age of twenty-one
were housed in New York's adult prisons, 800 were
fourteen or younger, and 175 were under the age of ten.

The need for a "Champion" for the children was immense. At the time, New York City's population was over five hundred thousand, and the Chief of Police, George W. Matsell, estimated there were ten thousand homeless children wandering the streets of New York. Other officials, at the same time, argued the figure was closer to thirty thousand.

In his concern for children, Charles Loring Brace visited many countries in Europe to study their solution for the homeless. When he returned to the United States, he was armed with many ideas that might lighten the social burden of this problem.

What the children had basic needs for, Brace felt, were education, jobs, and good homes. This was just what he would work to help provide for them through his newly organized Children's Aid Society which he helped to found in 1853.

He believed there was a way to change the futures of these children by removing them from poverty and placing them in "morally, upright farm families," where, he thought, they would have a "chance of escaping a lifetime of suffering and want."

Charles Loring Brace is credited with starting the institution of modern adoption in the United States. Brace, through the Children's Aid Society, sought out small towns, starting primarily in the Midwest, to place children in adoptive homes.

Brace's system of adoption and placing-out soon became widely known throughout the United States. By 1929, when the last Children's Aid Society train rolled west carrying orphans, no fewer than 150,000 children had found new homes and new lives.

Five Points

In the 1800s, a particularly dangerous location in New York City was where the streets of Worth, Baxter and Park intersected. Five Points was named for the points created by those intersecting streets. This location was known as a center of "vice and debauchery." It was such a dangerous place that no police officer would patrol the location without four other officers to accompany him; it was said that during the daylight hours to have been a row of "thieves, murderers, and homeless children."

The Five Points were described in 1842 by Charles Dickens who wrote: "This is the place: these narrow ways diverging to the right and left, and reeking every where with dirt and filth. Such lives as are led here, bear the same fruit here as elsewhere. The coarse and bloated faces at the doors have counterparts at home (London) and all the wide world over. Debauchery has made the very houses prematurely old. See how the rotten beams are tumbling down, and how the patched and broken windows seem to scowl dimly, like eyes that have been hurt in drunken frays. Many of these pigs live here. Do they ever wonder why their masters walk upright in lieu of going on all fours? and why they talk instead of grunting?"

Michigan Central Rail Road
1860 Advertisement

The Michigan Central Rail Road was originated
and partially built by the State of Michigan, and in the
year 1846, it was purchased by the Michigan Central
Company. This company has made marked improvements
in re-building and straightening the track, laying steel
rails completing the road to Chicago, and running the
first train from Detroit to Chicago on the 21st day of
June, 1852. The tracks are smooth and well ballasted,
making it one of the most desirable roads in the country
for travel. The bridges are all built of iron in an
exceptionally strong and substantial manner, making
them perfectly safe. This general statement of the
construction of this great trunk, which connects two
important metropolitan centers, may be accepted as a
brief and cursory statement of what would require a
ponderous volume to fairly express in detail, as the
values by the Michigan Central, whose appointments of
rolling stock, and whose superb arrangements for the
comfort of the traveling community cannot be excelled
by any of the rail road corporations in the country. The
engines used by the Michigan Central are first class with
all the modern improvements being tested satisfactorily
on a basis of strength, speed and safety. The luxurious
coaches are the acme of beauty and excellence, being
graded to compare with the most sumptuous in America,
the Premier Classe in France, or the English Coach.
They are insignificant when placed in comparison with
the gorgeous salons, boudoirs, and reception drawing
rooms of the Michigan Central Rail Road.

Faraway Home Time Line

1826: June 19, Charles Loring Brace is born in Litchfield, Connecticut.

Erie Canal opens as a gateway to the West.

1836: First mill built in Dowagiac, Michigan.

1837: Michigan becomes a state.

1842: Charles Loring Brace attends Yale University.

1848: February, Michigan Central Rail Road construction comes to Dowagiac.

Charles Loring Brace moves to New York City from Connecticut to study.

Ladies' Methodist Home Missionary Society locates across the street from the Brewery at Five Points.

1848-49: New York City cholera epidemic kills 5,071, one percent of the city's population.

1849: New York's first police chief, George Matsell, reports 3,000 homeless children living alone in the area of Five Points.

1850: Over 2,600,000 immigrants from Ireland and Germany enter the United States, primarily through New York.

New York City population reaches 500,000.

1851: 4,000 inmates under twenty-one years of age are in New York's adult prisons; 800 are fourteen or younger while 175 are under the age of ten.

1852: June 21, first Michigan Central Rail Road runs from Detroit to Chicago.

1853: January 9, Charles Loring Brace meets with investors and ministers to found the Children's Aid Society in New York.

First CAS office opens at 683 Broadway on the corner of Amity Street (Third Street).

1854: March, First Lodging House opens for homeless youth.

September 28: (Thursday) CAS orphans leave New York City heading toward Dowagiac, Michigan, aboard a steamship traveling on the Hudson River to Albany. Overnight travel.

September 29: (Friday) CAS orphans arrive in Albany in the early morning and leave for Buffalo, New York, aboard a train. Overnight travel.

September 30: (Saturday) CAS orphans arrive in Buffalo and board a ship crossing Lake Erie to Detroit. Overnight travel.

October 1: (Sunday) CAS orphans travel all day, still aboard the ship on Lake Erie, and arrive in Detroit at 10 pm, where they board the Michigan Central Rail Road in Detroit before midnight.

October 2: (Monday) CAS orphans arrive at Dowagiac, Michigan.

October 3: (Tuesday) Placement of children begins in Dowagiac. Fifteen children find immediate placement.

October 5: (Thursday) Rev. E. P. Smith leaves Dowagiac for Chicago with the children yet to be placed.

1863: Dowagiac incorporates as a village.

1876: CAS establishes the first recognized kindergarten in America.

1890: August 11, Charles Loring Brace dies.

1929: Last placement train travels to Trenton, Missouri. This is the last train because, by this time, the child labor laws and new welfare programs to help children are in place, and there are many established resources for the well-being of children and families. Thanks, in part, to Charles Loring Brace.

Glossary

barges: flat-bottom freight boats

basket-bottle: a basket that holds a bottle

benefactor: act of giving or doing something charitable

berths: a bunk or bed in a ship or train car

billy club: a handheld stick or club used by police

buggies: horse-drawn vehicles

bummer: a loafer or idler; a begger

castoff: something that has been thrown away

charity: the giving of aid to the poor

cheek-to-jowl: being very close; face-to-face

chew: chewing tobacco by-products

cipher: to do and understand mathematical problems

contraptions: inventions or modern machines

cur: a mongrel or inferior dog

dandy: fancy-dressed male

deloused: removal of lice

dung: manure

emigrant: someone who leaves one place to live in another

Five Points: dangerous location in the 1800s in New York City

Freight agent: someone who handles and manages freight boxes and shipping

gang: a group of people acting or organizing for a common cause

gangplank: a temporary bridge for getting on and off a vessel at dockside

gee: direction given to a horse by its driver meaning "turn right"

gruel: warm grain cooked similar to oatmeal

ghettoes: a section of a city, often run-down and overcrowded

Good Book: Bible

gorm: Irish expression of surprise

hamper: woven straw container to carry articles

haw: direction given to a horse by its driver meaning "turn left"

iron horse: train engine

lickety-split: as fast as possible

minister: leader of a church or religious order

naught: nothing

newsie: young boy who sells newspapers on the street

oratory: the art of public speaking

patron: one who protects, fosters or supports someone in need of aid

peach: someone who tells on someone else

planked sidewalk: a walkway made of wood

pratty: potato

privies: outhouse

pullcart: horseless cart pulled by hand

schooner: a fore-and-aft-rigged vessel generally having two or more masts

sentry: guard

side-wheeler: a boat with its paddle wheels located on the sides of the ship

shanghaied: slang for kidnapped

skitterish: jumpy or afraid

slops: a jar or bowl used to go to the bathroom in

snoozers: people who sleep on the streets

squalor: filth; degraded living conditions

steamship: a sailing vessel that derives its energy from steam

steerage: the lowest level of a ship where the steering mechanisms are located

substance: something that contains mass and density

tenant buildings: a building where one rents a space to live in

tender: wood-carrying train car that followed behind the train engine

tinker man: door-to-door salesman peddling his wares

vigil: an act or period of keeping awake or watching over

vocation: stated occupation

wee: very small

whoa: direction given a horse by its driver meaning "stop"

yacht: an expensive vessel propelled by sail or power and used for cruising or racing

Bibliography

BOOKS

Ackroyd, Peter. <u>Dickens</u>. New York: Harper Collins
Publishers, 1990.

Atwell, Willis. <u>Do You Know</u>. Booth Newspapers, Inc., 1937.

Boyer, Paul. <u>Urban Masses and Moral Order in America: 1820-
1920</u>. Cambridge, Mass: Harvard University Press, 1978.

Brace, Charles Loring. <u>The Dangerous Classes of New York and
Twenty Years' Work Among Them</u>. New York: Wynkoop &
Hallenbeck, Publishers, 1880.

Brace, Emma. <u>The Life of Charles Loring Brace Told Chiefly in
His Own Letters</u>. New York: Charles Scribner's Sons, 1894.

Bremner, Robert H., ed. <u>Children and Youth in America: A
Documentary History</u>. Vol. 3, Cambridge, Mass.: Harvard
University Press, 1970-74.

Coble, Janet M. <u>Children of Orphan Trains: From New York to
Illinois and Beyond</u>. Springfield, Illinois: Illinois State
Genealogical Society, 1994, 1997.

Del Vecchio, Mike. <u>Pictorial History of America's Railroads</u>.
New York: MBI Publishing Company, 1998.

Hamper, Stan. <u>Dowagiac Stories-Windows to the Past</u>.
Dowagiac Commercial Press, 1996.

Hartz, John Von. <u>New York Street Kids: 136 Photographs
Selected by The Children's Aid Society</u>. New York: Dover
Publications, Inc., 1978.

Hayes, Tadhg. The Wit of Irish Conversation. Dublin: O'Brien Press, 1996.

Holt, Marilyn Irvin. The Orphan Trains: Placing Out in America. University of Nebraska Press: Lincoln and London, 1949, 1992, 1994.

Ingham, Patricia, ed. Dickens, Charles American Notes for General Circulation. Penguin Books, 2000.

Jackson, Kenneth T., ed. The Encyclopedia of New York City. New Haven, Conn.: Yale University Press.

Johnson, Mary Ellen, and Kay B. Hall, eds. Orphan Train Riders: Their Own Stories. Volumes I and II. Baltimore, Md.: Gateway Press, 1992, 1993.

Johnson, Mary Ellen, ed. Orphan Train Riders: Their Own Stories. Vols. 1-4, Baltimore: Gateway Press, 1992-97.

Katz, Michael B. In the Shadow of the Poorhouse: A Social History of Welfare in America. New York: Basic Books, Inc., Publishers, 1986.

Knitzer, Jane, Mary Lee Allen, and Brenda McGowan. Children Without Homes: An Examination of Public Responsibility to Children in Out-of-Home Care. Washington, D.C.: Children's Defense Fund.

Kosky, Jules. Mutual Friends: Charles Dickens and Great Ormond Street Children's Hospital. New York: St. Martin's Press, 1989.

Langsam, Miriam Z. Children West: A History of the Placing-Out System of the New York Children's Aid Society, 1853-1890. Madison: State Historical Society for the Department of History, University of Wisconsin, 1964.

Nasaw, David. <u>Children of the City: At Work and At Play</u>. New York: Oxford University Press, 1985.

O'Connor, Stephen. <u>The Story of Charles Loring Brace and the Children He Saved and Failed</u>. Boston and New York: Houghton Mifflin Company, 2001.

Pollock, Linda A. <u>Forgotten Children: Parent-Child Relation from 1500 to 1900</u>. Cambridge University Press, 1983.

Riis, Jacob A. <u>How the Other Half Lives</u>. New York: Charles Scribner's Sons, 1890.

Singer, Eliot and Lockwood, R. Yvonne. <u>Michigan in Song: Traditional and Contemporary Songs of Michigan</u>. East Lansing, Michigan, Michigan Traditional Arts Program, Michigan State University Museum, 1990.

Spann, Edward K. <u>The New Metropolis: New York City, 1840-1857</u>. New York: Columbia University Press, 1981.

Tayler, Arthur. <u>History of North American Railroads: from 1830 to the Present Day</u>. Edison, New Jersey: Chartwell Books, Inc., 1996.

Warren, Andrea. <u>Orphan Train Rider: One Boy's True Story</u>. Boston, Houghton Mifflin Company, 1996.

Youcha, Geraldine. <u>Minding the Children: Child Care in America from Colonial Times to the Present</u>. New York: Charles Scribner's Sons, 1995.

Zelizer, Viviana A. <u>Pricing the Priceless Child: The Changing Social Value of Children</u>. New York: Basic Books, Inc., 1985.

<u>The Children's Aid Society of New York: Its Emigration or Placing Out System and Its Results</u>. Privately Published by the Children's Aid Society, 1910.

196

Magazines

Fry, Annette Riley. "The Children's Migration." *The American Heritage Magazine,* December 1974, 4-10.

Newspapers/Articles Online

An Act of Love by Rev. Kenneth Krueger:
http://www.lutheransforlife.org/Life%20Issue%20Info/Adoption/An_Act_of_Love.htm

Champion of Children: Charles Loring Brace:
http://www.childabuse.org/champions2.htm

Charles Loring Brace, "The Life of the Street Rats" 1872:
http://occawlonline.pearsoned.com/bookbind/pubbooks/nash5e_awl/medialib/timeline/docs/sources/theme_primarysources_Labor_3.html

Dowagiac, City of: http://www.cityofdowagiac.com

Orphan Trains of Kansas by Connie DiPasquale:
http://www.kancoll.org/articles/orphans

Orphan Train Stories:
http://www.rotsweb.com/~neadoptn/Orphan.htm

The American Experience/The Orphan Trains:
http://www.pbs.org/wgbh/amex/orphan/orphants.html

The Children's Aid Society:
http://www.childrensaidsociety.org

The Orphan Train in Michigan by Al Eicher Lakeshore Guardian:
http://www.lakeshoreguardian.com/_2002/062002/

The Orphan Trains of Charles Loring Brace by Stephen O'Connor: http://www.nytimes.com/books/first/o/oconnor-01orphan.html

They Rode the Orphan Trains by Jim McCarty: http://www.rootsweb.com/~mogrundy/orphans.html

Westward Ho! All Aboard the Orphan Train by Meg Greene Malvasi: http://www.suite101.com/article.cfm/history_for_children/18536

Societies

The Orphan Train Heritage Society of America
614 East Ema Ave.
Suite 115
Springdale, AZ 72764

New England Home for Little Wanders
850 Boylston Street
Boston, MA 02167

New York Foundling Hospital
590 Avenue of the Americas
New York, NY 10017

Children's Village
Dobbs Ferry, NY 10522

Songs

"Come Ye Sinners Poor and Needy" by Joseph Hart, 1759

"Michigan," Anonymous